实用导游英语

(社会与文化)

(第二版)

Practical Tour Guiding English
(Chinese Society & Local Culture)

(The Second Edition)

主　编　王向宁
编　委　韩　鸽　徐明宇　张　敏　冯　蕾
　　　　姚天洋　张艳妍　栗　娜　甄　真
　　　　彭洪明　曹宪荣　李　杰
主　审　〔美〕W. Daniel Garst　〔美〕Leo (Liu Zhigang)

图书在版编目(CIP)数据

实用导游英语. 社会与文化/王向宁主编. —2版. —北京:北京大学出版社,2014.5
(21世纪旅游英语系列教材)
ISBN 978-7-301-24125-7

Ⅰ.①实… Ⅱ.①王… Ⅲ.①导游—英语—高等职业教育—教材 Ⅳ.①H31

中国版本图书馆CIP数据核字(2014)第072559号

书　　　　名:	**实用导游英语(社会与文化)(第二版)**
著作责任者:	王向宁　主编
责 任 编 辑:	刘　爽　叶　丹
标 准 书 号:	ISBN 978-7-301-24125-7/H·3504
出 版 发 行:	北京大学出版社
地　　　　址:	北京市海淀区成府路205号　100871
网　　　　址:	http://www.pup.cn　新浪官方微博:@北京大学出版社
电　　　　话:	邮购部 62752015　发行部 62750672　编辑部 62759634　出版部 62754962
电 子 信 箱:	nkliushuang@hotmail.com
印　刷　者:	北京大学印刷厂
经　销　者:	新华书店
	787毫米×980毫米　16开本　14印张　200千字
	2010年11月第1版
	2014年5月第2版　2018年9月第3次印刷
定　　　　价:	35.00元

未经许可,不得以任何方式复制或抄袭本书之部分或全部内容。
版权所有,侵权必究
举报电话: 010-62752024　电子信箱: fd@pup.pku.edu.cn

ACKNOWLEDGEMENTS

The aim of this textbook is to introduce tourism English and professional tour guiding knowledge and skills to Chinese readers and students. We are indebted to many sources for the passages and pictures selected for reading. With regard to the issue of copyright, we have made extensive efforts to contact the publishers and authors of these passages and pictures, but for various reasons we have been unable to establish communication in some cases. In these cases we apologize to the publishers and authors in advance and will be happy to make fuller acknowledgement in due course. For any questions concerning copyright and permissions, please contact.

Telephone: +86 10 65778276
E-mail: willarr@126.com

We will be happy to make any necessary arrangements for the appropriate settlement of any possible copyright issues.

前　言

《实用导游英语》是面向全国高等院校旅游专业和旅游职高学生编写的专业英语教材，同时也可供旅游业从业人员和外事接待人员作为自学教材和工具书。

本教材在构架、内容、编排等方面做了大胆创新。从导游人员应具备的基本知识和语言技能出发，力求整套教材结构合理，内容具备实用性和针对性。

本套教材分为"风景名胜"和"社会与文化"两分册。"风景名胜"分册系统地介绍了我国的故都风貌、名山大川、宗教圣地、海滨胜地、丝绸之路、草原湖泊、陵墓园林、主题公园、溶洞和瀑布、人间仙境及香港、澳门特别行政区和我国台湾地区等。"社会与文化"分册则介绍了我国的风俗民情、传统节日、饮食文化、饮茶品酒、戏曲杂技、建筑风格、宗教信仰、传统医学、民间传说、精华国粹、特殊兴趣旅游及新兴业态等。课文选材注意典型性和代表性，内容上注意重点突出，既强调特色又详略得当，以期学生可以触类旁通、举一反三。两分册可单独使用，配合使用效果更佳。

本套教材的另一特色是在每个单元后都独立设计有一个"导游技巧和业务"板块。该板块由导游业务知识和技巧、实操性练习、案例分析三部分构成，旨在让读者了解导游工作中常见问题的预防和处理技巧。

为加强听说能力的训练和感官体验，本套教材每个单元还设计了"听说板块"和"视频板块"。"听说板块"由两篇与旅游相关的听力材料、与单元主题相关的课堂讨论和小组活动构成。"视频板块"则一方面是单元主题内容的实景展示，另一方面还增加和拓展了相关知识。这两个板块的听力录音和视频可到北京大学出版社网站www.pup.cn下载。

为了增加活泼性和趣味性，提高学生的学习兴趣，每篇课文都配有与主题相关的精美图片。

本教材在编写过程中，参考了一些出版物和网站（详见参考文献）。由于选材广泛，书中没有一一注明出处，希望得到原作者的支持和谅解，并接受我们诚挚的谢意！此外，为了使学生有一个直观、感性的认识，并使版面活泼轻松，我们采用了一些公开发表的图片。由于部分图片无法联系到原作者，所以敬请原作者和读者见谅！

实 用 导 游 英 语

本教材在编写过程中承蒙中国旅游研究院院长戴斌教授、北京第二外国语学院旅游研究院院长张辉教授的大力支持和帮助,在此表示衷心感谢。

本套教材的修订版由来自北京第二外国语学院应用英语学院、中瑞酒店管理学院、中国国际旅行社的多位编者共同完成,他们是:王向宁、韩鸽、徐明宇、冯蕾、栗娜、甄真、彭洪明、张敏、姚天洋、张艳妍、曹宪荣、李杰。

由于时间仓促,本教材难免有疏漏不足之处,恳请广大读者批评指正。

王向宁
2014.1

目 录

Contents

Unit 1　General Introduction to China 中国概况 ·················· 1
  Text　　☞Text A　Chinese Population　中国人口　2
  　　　　☞Text B　Chinese Geography　中国地理　4
  　　　　☞Text C　Fifty-Six Ethnic Groups in China 56个民族　6
  Exercises 练习　9
  Professional Tour Guiding Knowledge & Skills　13
  　　导游技巧和业务：导游服务
  Case Study 案例分析　16
  拓展视频　16

Unit 2　Traditional Festivals 传统节日 ·················· 17
  Text　　☞Text A　The Spring Festival　春节　18
  　　　　☞Text B　The Dragon Boat Festival　端午节　20
  　　　　☞Text C　The Chinese Moon Festival　中秋节　22
  Exercises 练习　24
  Professional Tour Guiding Knowledge & Skills　28
  　　导游技巧和业务：导游服务技能
  Case Study 案例分析　31
  拓展视频　31

Unit 3　Local Customs 各地民俗 ·················· 32
  Text　　☞Text A　Ice and Snow Sculpture Festival　冰雕节　33
  　　　　☞Text B　Nadam Fair　那达慕　34
  　　　　☞Text C　Water Splashing Festival　泼水节　36
  Exercises 练习　38
  Professional Tour Guiding Knowledge & Skills　42
  　　导游技巧和业务：导游讲解技能
  Case Study 案例分析　44
  拓展视频　45

Unit 4　Chinese Cuisine 中国饮食文化 ················· 46

Text　　☞Text A　Chinese Cuisines 中国菜系　47
　　　　☞Text B　Beijing Roast Duck 北京烤鸭　49
　　　　☞Text C　Hot Pot 火锅　50

Exercises 练习　52

Professional Tour Guiding Knowledge & Skills　56
　导游技巧和业务：旅游者个别要求

Case Study 案例分析　59

拓展视频　59

Unit 5　Tea and Wine 饮茶品酒 ················· 60

Text　　☞Text A　Tea in China 中国茶　61
　　　　☞Text B　Chinese Wine 中国酒　63
　　　　☞Text C　Chinese Table Manners 中国餐桌礼仪　65

Exercises 练习　67

Professional Tour Guiding Knowledge & Skills　71
　导游技巧和业务：特殊旅游者的接待

Case Study 案例分析　74

拓展视频　75

Unit 6　Operas and Acrobatics 戏曲和杂技 ················· 76

Text　　☞Text A　Beijing Opera 京剧　77
　　　　☞Text B　Kunqu Opera 昆曲　79
　　　　☞Text C　Wuqiao 吴桥杂技　80

Exercises 练习　83

Professional Tour Guiding Knowledge & Skills　87
　导游技巧和业务：问题与事故处理

Case Study 案例分析　89

拓展视频　89

Unit 7　Architecture 建筑风格 ················· 90

Text　　☞Text A　Siheyuan 四合院　91
　　　　☞Text B　Tulou in Fujian Province 福建土楼　92
　　　　☞Text C　Residences of Southern Anhui 皖南民居　94

Exercises 练习　96
Professional Tour Guiding Knowledge & Skills　100
　　导游技巧和业务：投诉处理
Case Study 案例分析　102
拓展视频　102

Unit 8　Religion 宗教信仰 ································· 103

Text　☞Text A　Buddhism 佛教　104
　　　☞Text B　Taoism 道家　106
　　　☞Text C　Islam 伊斯兰教　108
Exercises 练习　110
Professional Tour Guiding Knowledge & Skills　114
　　导游技巧和业务：法定标识
Case Study 案例分析　117
拓展视频　117

Unit 9　Traditional Chinese Medicine 中医 ················· 118

Text　☞Text A　Traditional Chinese Medicine 中医　119
　　　☞Text B　Chinese Acupuncture 针灸　121
　　　☞Text C　Chinese Herbal Medicine 中草药　123
Exercises 练习　125
Professional Tour Guiding Knowledge & Skills　129
　　导游技巧和业务：航空知识
Case Study 案例分析　132
拓展视频　132

Unit 10　Folklore 民间传说 ································ 133

Text　☞Text A　Cowherd and Weaving Girl 牛郎织女　134
　　　☞Text B　Meng Jiangnv 孟姜女　135
　　　☞Text C　Legend of Chang E 嫦娥奔月　137
Exercises 练习　140
Professional Tour Guiding Knowledge & Skills　144
　　导游技巧和业务：出入境知识
Case Study 案例分析　147
拓展视频　147

Unit 11 Quintessence of Chinese Culture 精华国粹 ·················· 148

 Text ☞Text A Chinese Calligraphy 书法　149
     ☞Text B Wushu (Martial Arts) 武术　151
     ☞Text C Mahjong 麻将　153
 Exercises 练习　155
 Professional Tour Guiding Knowledge & Skills　159
  导游技巧和业务：货币知识
 Case Study 案例分析　162
 拓展视频　162

Unit 12 Special Interest Tourism 特殊兴趣旅游 ·················· 163

 Text ☞Text A Tours by Interest　兴趣之旅　164
     ☞Text B Adventure Tourism　探险旅游　166
     ☞Text C Photography Tourism　摄影旅游　168
 Exercises 练习　170
 Professional Tour Guiding Knowledge & Skills　174
  导游技巧和业务：跨文化意识
 Case Study 案例分析　177
 拓展视频　177

Unit 13 Emerging Tourism 新兴旅游 ·················· 178

 Text ☞Text A Red Tourism 红色旅游　179
     ☞Text B Rural Tourism 乡村旅游　181
     ☞Text C Health and Wellness Tourism 养生旅游　183
 Exercises 练习　185
 Professional Tour Guiding Knowledge & Skills　189
  导游技巧和业务：新旅游法
 Case Study 案例分析　192
 拓展视频 192

练习参考答案 ·················· 193
参考书目 ·················· 211

Unit 1 General Introduction to China

▶▶ 导读

中国,又称华夏、神州、九州,有着五千多年的悠久历史,与古埃及、古巴比伦、古印度并列为"世界四大文明古国"。中国地大物博,陆地面积约960万平方公里;人口超过13亿;有56个民族,统称为中华民族。龙是中华民族的象征。

WARM-UP QUESTIONS

Historically speaking, China has always been a populous country with a vast territory. On this beautiful land there have lived many ethnic groups. Do you know which ethnic group the following people belong to? What do you know about these ethnic minorities? Talk about it with your partners.

Text A

Chinese Population

China is the world's most populous country with 1.36 billion at the end of 2013, accounting for one-fifth of the total global population. This figure does not include the Chinese living in the Hong Kong and Macao Special Administrative Regions, and Taiwan region. As a result, although China has the third largest territory in the world, the population density is about 142 per square kilometer, roughly four times greater than that of the US.① Most of the population of China live in the middle and lower reaches of the Yellow River, Yangtze River and Pearl River valleys, and the Northeast Plain.②

According to the traditional Chinese beliefs of family, more children mean greater happiness and a bigger fortune. Consequently, China had always boasted a relatively larger population than other countries throughout history. After the foundation of New China in 1949, the population grew rapidly due to the stable social situation, the rapid increase in production across all sectors of the national economy, as well as improved medical and health conditions.③ The government at first was not fully aware of the importance of population control. By the end of 1969, Chinese population had already reached 806.71 million.

Fortunately, in the early 1970s, the Chinese government realized that the boomimg population was harmful to economic and social development and would put great pressure on employment, housing, communications and medical care and the like.④ The leaders began to understand that if the over-rapid population growth could not be effectively reversed, it would probably endanger the necessary conditions for the survival of humanity, along with China's sustainable social and economic development⑤. Then the Chinese government began implementing a policy of family planning, population control, and population quality improvement. These measures accorded with China's basic conditions of being a large country with a poor economic

Vocabulary
populous 人口众多的
density 密度
communication 通信
reverse 倒转
endanger 危及
survival 生存
humanity 人类

Unit 1 General Introduction to China

foundation, particularly its large population and limited amount of arable land, so as to promote the development of the economy, society, resources and environment.⑥ The basic requirements of family planning are late marriages and late childbearing. The aim is to have fewer but healthier babies; couples are limited to have just one child. At the same time, a flexible family planning policy has been adopted for rural people and ethnic minorities. This is especially the case for minorities: each ethnic group may work out different regulations according to its own wishes, population, natural resources, economy, culture and customs.⑦

Since then birth rates have steadily declined year by year. China's birth rate dropped from 34.11 per thousand in 1969 to 12.08 per thousand by the end of 2013; at the same time, the natural growth rate decreased from 26.08 per thousand to 4.92 per thousand, thus basically realizing a change in the population reproduction type to the one characterized by low birth and death rates and a low population growth rate.⑧

> arable 适于耕种的
> childbearing 生育
> flexible 灵活的
> rural 农村的
> reproduction 繁殖

Notes

1. As a result, although China has the third largest territory in the world, the population density is about 142 per square kilometer, roughly four times greater than that of the US. 因此,尽管中国拥有世界第三大面积的领土,人口密度却达到134人/平方公里,大约为美国的四倍。

2. Most of the population of China live in the middle and lower reaches of the Yellow River, Yangtze River and Pearl River valleys, and the Northeast Plain. 中国的大部分人口生活在黄河流域、长江流域和珠江河谷以及东北平原地区。

3. After the foundation of New China in 1949, the population grew rapidly due to the stable social situation, the rapid increase in production across all sectors of the national economy, as well as improved medical and health conditions. 在1949年新中国成立之后,由于社会稳定、国民经济各部门生产的快速发展以及医疗健康水平的提高,中国人口快速增长。

4. Fortunately, in the early 1970s, the Chinese government realized that the booming population was harmful to economic and social development and would put great pressure on employment, housing, communications and medical care, and the like. 幸运的是,在20世纪70年代初期,中国政府意识到人口的迅速增长会对经济和社会的发展造成危害,也会给就业、住房、通信和医疗等方面造成巨大压力。

5. sustainable social and economic development 社会和经济的可持续发展

6. These measures accorded with China's basic conditions of being a large country with a poor economic foundation, particularly its large population and limited amount of arable land, so as to promote the development of the economy, society, resources and environment. 这些措施符合中国作为一个经济基础薄弱的大国的基本国情，特别是符合中国人口众多而耕地有限的情况，能够促进经济、社会、资源和环境等方面的发展。

   accord with 符合，一致

   e.g. What you have just said does not accord with what you told us yesterday.你刚才说的和你昨天告诉我们的不一样。

7. This is especially the case for minorities: each ethnic group may work out different regulations according to its own wishes, population, natural resources, economy, culture and customs. 特别是对于少数民族，每个少数民族都可以依据自身的意愿、人口数量、自然资源、经济条件、文化和习俗等各方面的情况制定出不同的制度。

8. ...basically realizing a change in the population reproduction type to the one characterized by low birth and death rates and a low population growth rate. 基本实现了人口生育类型的转变，成为低出生率、低死亡率和低增长率的社会。

Text B

Chinese Geography

Located in the eastern part of the Asian continent and western shore of the Pacific Ocean, People's Republic of China occupies a landmass of 9.6 million square kilometers, and is the third largest country in the world, next only to Russia and Canada. The Chinese territory comprises about 6.5 percent of the world total land area. It is predicted by World Travel Organization that by the year 2020, China will become the world's number one travel destination.

From north to south, the territory of China measures about 5,500 kilometers, stretching from the center of the Heilongjiang River, north of the town of Mohe to the Zengmu Reef① at the southernmost tip of the Nansha Islands. When North China is still covered with snow, people in the South China are busy with spring plowing. From west to east, the nation extends about 5,200 kilometers from the Pamirs② to the confluence of the Heilongjiang and Wusuli Rivers③, with a time difference of over four hours. When the Pamirs are cloaked in night, the morning sun is shining brightly over East China. With a land boundary of some 22,800

Vocabulary

landmass 大陆
plowing 耕作
confluence 汇合
cloak 掩盖
boundary 边界

Unit 1 General Introduction to China

kilometers and a sea boundary of more than 18,000 kilometers, China has more neighbors than any other countries in the world, with a total of 20 contiguous countries.

Topographically speaking, the terrain gradually descends from west to east like a staircase. The Qinghai-Tibet Plateau, averaging more than 4,000 meters above sea level, is called "the roof of the world". ④ When taking a bird's-eye view of China, it is easy to figure out that China is basically a mountainous country, with two-thirds of its total land area covered by mountains, hills and high plateaus. Seven of the world's twelve highest peaks exceeding 8,000 meters in height are located in China. Mount Everest⑤, the highest peak in China, is also the highest in the world.

The eastern part of China is flanked by the Pacific. More than 5,000 islands have scattered over a spectacular area of the sea, with Taiwan Island as the largest. China abounds in rivers. The inland river system accounts for 36 percent of the total land area in China. The Yangtze River, with a total length of 6,300 kilometers, is the longest river in China and the third

longest in the world. This artery course through several of China's most economically developed regions. ⑥ Excellent river ports—Shanghai, Nanjing, Wuhan, and Chongqing—are located along this river, making it one of the world's busiest inland waterways. ⑦ The Yellow River is the second longest river in China. It's said that the Chinese civilization was born just along this river, which has won the river the fame of "the Mother River" of the Chinese nation. The two rivers, as well as the Pearl River in South China, have provided the framework for agricultural development and population growth throughout Chinese history. ⑧

contiguous 毗邻的
topographically 地形学地
descend 下降
bird's-eye 鸟瞰的
exceed 超过
flank 在……的侧面
spectacular 壮观的
artery 动脉，要道
waterway 水路
framework 框架

实用导游英语

Notes

1. Zengmu Reef 曾母暗沙，位于南沙群岛南端，是中国领土的最南点，形如纺锤，为水下珊瑚礁，面积21.2平方公里。
2. Pamirs 帕米尔高原，古称不周山，汉代后称葱岭，位于中亚东南部、中国的西端，目前除东部倾斜坡归中国管辖外，大部分属于塔吉克斯坦，只有瓦罕帕米尔属阿富汗。
3. the confluence of the Heilongjiang and Wusuli Rivers 黑龙江和乌苏里江的交汇处
4. The Qinghai-Tibet Plateau, averaging more than 4,000 meters above sea level, is called "the roof of the world". 青藏高原，平均海拔4000米以上，素有"世界屋脊"之称。
5. Mount Everest 珠穆朗玛峰，是喜马拉雅山的主峰，海拔8844.43米，为地球上第一高峰，地处中国和尼泊尔边界东段，北坡位于中国境内。藏语称"珠穆朗玛"，意为"神女第三"。
6. This artery course through several of China's most economically developed regions. 这条水路流经中国几个经济最发达的地区。
7. Excellent river ports—Shanghai, Nanjing, Wuhan, and Chongqing—are located along this river, making it one of the world's busiest inland waterways. 几个优良的河流港口——上海、南京、武汉和重庆——都分布在这条河流的沿岸，这使它成为世界上最繁忙的内河水路之一。
8. The two rivers, as well as the Pearl River in South China, have provided the framework for agricultural development and population growth throughout Chinese history. 这两条河，同南方的珠江一道，在中国的历史上，一直为农业的发展和人口的增长提供基本的框架。

Text C

Fifty-Six Ethnic Groups in China

From the hinterlands of the north, to the lush jungles in the south, from the mountains of Taiwan in the east, to the top of the world in the west, China serves as home to 56 officially registered ethnic groups. The largest group, the Han, makes up over 91.6% of China's vast population, and it is the elements of Han civilization that the world considers the main body of "Chinese culture". Yet, the 55 ethnic minorities, making up the remaining 8.4% according to the Fifth National Population Census in 2000, maintain their own rich traditions and customs, and all are part of Chinese culture.

With a population of 1,159.4 million, the Han Chinese can be found in almost every part of China. They form the largest ethnic group within China and also the largest in the world. The Han nationality uses

Vocabulary
hinterland 穷乡僻壤
jungle 丛林
census 人口普查

Unit 1 General Introduction to China

its own spoken and written language, known as the Chinese language, which has been and is currently used all over China and is one of the working languages of the United Nations. The Han culture belongs to one of the world's oldest civilizations, boasting a lot of outstanding achievements in many fields including politics, military affairs, philosophy, literature, art and natural science.①

The 55 ethnic minorities, though fewer in number, are distributed over some 50% of Chinese territory mostly in border areas. The largest is the 16 million-strong Zhuang in Southwestern China.② Most of the 55 ethnic minorities use their own languages. They have developed individual customs regarding food, clothing and etiquette, in response to their own particular environments, social conditions and

levels of economic development.③ Many of the minorities have their own religious beliefs. For example, the Hui, Uigur, together with some other peoples, adhere to Islam; the Tibetans and Mongolians follow Tibetan Buddhism; and the Dai, Blang and Deang to Hinayana Buddhism.④ Chinese government has respected their religious beliefs and made efforts to preserve their religious freedom.

Chinese government has made equality, unity, mutual help and common prosperity as its basic principles in handling the relations between ethnic groups.⑤ Accordingly, China has practised a regional ethnic autonomy system in which autonomous organs of self-government are established under the unified leadership of the central government.⑥ The minority people exercise autonomous rights, and are masters in their own region and administer their own internal affairs. By now, China has five Autonomous Regions for its minorities: Guangxi, Xinjiang, Tibet, Inner Mongolia and Ningxia.⑦ Since many minorities reside in the remote areas and are usually poor, Chinese government has instituted preferential policies to provide training and other aid for the minorities to progress, govern and manage their lives⑧.

distribute 分布
etiquette 礼节
adhere 坚持
Islam 伊斯兰教
Tibetan Buddhism 藏传佛教
Blang 布朗族
Deang 德昂族
Hinayana Buddhism 小乘佛教
prosperity 繁荣
autonomy 自治
organ 机关
self-government 自治
reside 居住

7

Notes

1. The Han culture belongs to one of the world's oldest civilizations, boasting a lot of outstanding achievements in many fields including politics, military affairs, philosophy, literature, art and natural science. 汉族文化属于世界上最古老的文明之一，在包括政治、军事、哲学、文学、艺术和自然科学等很多领域中拥有众多杰出的成就。

2. The largest is the 16 million-strong Zhuang in Southwestern China. 最大的（少数民族）是居住在西南部的壮族（主要聚居在广西、云南等地，人口超过1600万人）。

3. They have developed individual customs regarding food, clothing and etiquette, in response to their own particular environments, social conditions and levels of economic development. 根据各自所处的环境、社会条件和经济发展水平，各少数民族都形成了各自饮食、着装和礼节等方面的风俗。

4. Many of the minorities have their own religious beliefs. For example, the Hui, Uigur, together with some other peoples, adhere to Islam; the Tibetans and Mongolians follow Tibetan Buddhism; and the Dai, Blang and Deang to Hinayana Buddhism. 许多少数民族都拥有自己的宗教信仰。例如，回族、维吾尔族以及其他一些少数民族信仰伊斯兰教；藏族和蒙古族信仰藏传佛教；而傣族、布朗族和德昂族信奉小乘佛教。

5. Chinese government has made equality, unity, mutual help and common prosperity as its basic principles in handling the relations between ethnic groups. 中国政府将平等、团结、互助和共同繁荣作为处理民族关系问题的基本原则。

6. Accordingly, China has practised a regional ethnic autonomy system in which autonomous organs of self-government are established under the unified leadership of the central government. 因此，中国实施了区域民族自治的行政体系，在中央政府的统一领导之下，建立了民族自治的政府机构。

7. By now, China has five Autonomous Regions for its minorities: Guangxi, Xinjiang, Tibet, Inner Mongolia and Ningxia. 现在，中国共有五个民族自治区：广西壮族自治区、新疆维吾尔族自治区、西藏自治区、内蒙古自治区以及宁夏回族自治区。

8. Chinese government has instituted preferential policies to provide training and other aid for the minorities to progress, govern and manage the lives 中国政府对少数民族地区施行特惠政策，为其提供各种培训及帮助，以帮助少数民族人民不断进步、更好地统辖和管理民族地区

Useful Phrases and Expressions

1. be aware of 知道，认识到
2. family planning 计划生育
3. accord with 符合
4. be located in 位于
5. the roof of the world 世界屋脊
6. abound in 富于
7. ethnic minority 少数民族
8. in response to 相应，适应
9. autonomous rights 自治权利

Unit 1 General Introduction to China

Exercises

Part I *Listening Practice*

Passage 1

Tourist Industry Lowering Prices

pummel 打击
consecutive 连续的
tour operator 包价旅游承办商
wondrous 令人惊奇的
outbreak 爆发

blizzard 大风雪
discount 折扣
recoup 补偿
off-season 淡季的

Task 1 Listen to the passage carefully and then fill in the blanks with what you hear. The passage will be read only once.

Top scenic spots in southern China have lowered prices to ____1____ to areas pummeled by blizzards in January and February.

Some scenic spots received no visitors for ____2____ days during and after the worst weather in 50 years, while many others suffered ____3____ in business. The total loss across the country is estimated at ____4____, according to the China National Tourism Administration (CNTA).

Many scenic spots are offering attractive ____5____ to individual tourists and favorable policies to ____6____ in a bid to recoup the losses. Hunan Province's Zhangjiajie, the UNESCO World Heritage site famous for its ____7____, said it would prolong its ____8____ favoring tour group operators until the end of the month, four weeks longer than usual. Huangshan, in Anhui Province, cut the off-season entrance fee from ____9____ to 100 Yuan in February. The price-cut has worked. Most tourists who came shortly after the disaster are from neighboring cities.

A senior official with the CNTA said the disaster dealt "another heavy blow to

实 用 导 游 英 语

China's tourism" five years after the SARS ___10___. Infrastructure can be repaired in a short period of time, but some natural sceneries are unlikely to be restored for a while.

Task 2 Listen to the recording again and then answer the following questions.

(1) What happened in January and February?

(2) What did the scenic spots decide to do in order to recoup the losses?

(3) Where were the visitors who came shortly after the disaster from?

(4) What have been the heavy blows to China's tourism in recent years?

(5) What is the biggest problem for these scenic spots now?

Passage 2

Rising RMB Boosts Hong Kong Tour

exchange rate 汇率
cosmetic 化妆品
tour package 包办旅游
Lantern Festival 元宵节
peg 把价格限定在某一范围内
travel agency 旅行社
Labor Law 劳动法

Unit 1 General Introduction to China

Task 1 Listen to the passage carefully and then fill in the blanks with what you hear. The passage will be read only once.

As the US dollar exchange rate to RMB declines, RMB's value against Hong Kong dollar, which is ____1____ to the dollar, also rises. RMB's rising value has started to bring ____2____ on the Hong Kong ____3____ since many mainlanders are now considering a tour to Hong Kong. In Shenzhen and Dongguan, two cities in south China's Guangdong Province, the number of people registering for Hong Kong tour has increased a little bit recently.

Based on the recent exchange rate, a cosmetics product sold at 630 Yuan in Hong Kong last year is now worth around ____4____ Yuan. Last year, mainlanders might pay ____5____ for every 10,000 Hong Kong dollars and now, it will save them 600-some Yuan to exchange for the same amount. Because of this ____6____ of Hong Kong dollar, many people in the mainland want to travel to Hong Kong at this time.

Some travel agencies in Shenzhen also include ____7____ in their tour package. More and more people make calls to the travel agencies for information and the number of people registering for Hong Kong tours has increased by ____8____ over last year. Some travel agencies have started to offer a higher price for ____9____ and they might not lower the price of outbound tours until the exchange rate remain ____10____ , said these travel agencies.

Task 2 What is exchange rate in your opinion? What are the advantages and challenges Chinese people would face as RMB rises? Talk about these two questions with your partners.

Part II Oral Practice

Task 1 Group Discussion

The class will be divided into three large groups, each of which will focus on one of the three aspects of China talked in this unit, namely, population, geography and ethnic nationalities. You can use all the materials that are available to you. Then select some representatives to report to the class.

Task 2　Role Play

Work in groups of 4 or 5. One of you is a tour guide. The rest are foreign visitors who are on the first day of their first visit to China, so they are eager to understand everything about China. The tour guide would use all his or her knowledge, especially what they have learned in this unit to cope with their endless questions. It is very important for a tour guide to be informative and patient.

Part III　Translation

Task 1　Translate the following words or phrases into English.

(1) 地大物博　　　　　　(2) 共同繁荣
(3) 物产丰富　　　　　　(4) 人杰地灵
(5) 可持续发展　　　　　(6) 人口密度
(7) 优惠政策　　　　　　(8) 珠穆朗玛峰
(9) 全国人口普查　　　　(10) 统一的多民族国家

Task 2　Translate the following paragraph into English.

从20世纪70年代以来,中国政府坚持不懈地在全国范围推行计划生育基本国策,鼓励晚婚晚育,提倡一对夫妻生育一个孩子。经过30年的艰苦努力,中国在经济还不发达的情况下,有效地控制了人口过快增长,实现了人口再生产类型向低出生率、低死亡率、低自然增长率的历史性转变,有力地促进了中国综合国力的提高、社会的进步和人民生活的改善,对稳定世界人口做出了积极的贡献。

Task 3　Translate the following paragraph into Chinese.

The geography of China stretches some 5,026 kilometers across the East Asian landmass bordering the East China Sea, Yellow Sea, and South China Sea, and between North Korea and Vietnam in a changing configuration of broad plains, expansive deserts, and lofty mountain ranges, including vast areas of inhospitable terrain (无人荒地).

Unit 1 General Introduction to China

导游技巧和业务
Professional Tour Guiding Knowledge & Skills

导游服务

导游服务范围
☞ 导游讲解服务
- 主要包括沿途讲解、参观游览景点的导游讲解以及为座谈、会见、交流、参观访问提供的各种导游讲解服务。

☞ 旅行生活服务
- 主要包括游客出入境迎送、旅途生活照料、安全服务及上下站联络等。

☞ 市内交通服务
- 是指导游同时兼任驾驶员,为游客在市内和市郊旅行游览时提供的开车服务。这种服务在西方旅游发达国家比较多见,目前在我国还极为少见。

导游服务特点
☞ 独立性强
- 独立宣传、执行国家政策 (national policy);
- 独立组织、协调旅游活动;
- 独立解决矛盾和处理突发性事件。

☞ 脑体高度结合
- 脑力劳动:导游需要有广博的知识面,古今中外、天文地理、政治、经济、社会、文化、医疗、卫生、宗教、民俗等均需涉猎。进行景观讲解、解答游客问题,这是一项复杂的脑力劳动;
- 体力劳动:带领游客游览,讲解介绍;还要随时随地帮助游客解决问题,事无巨细;尤其是旅游旺季时,工作连轴转,体力消耗大。

☞ 复杂多变
- 游客背景复杂,需求多种多样;
- 接触的人员多,人际关系复杂;
- 讲解内容庞杂、多变;
- 要面对各种物质诱惑和精神污染。

☞ 涉及面广
- 涉及的部门和单位多;

- 涉及知识技能领域广,如天文地理、花鸟虫鱼、文化艺术、名人轶事。这样才能提供内容丰富、言之有理、言之有据的讲解。

☞ 关联度高、责任大
- 旅游活动环环相扣,涉及众多部门和单位,需要导游从中衔接。

☞ 政策性强
- 应正确处理涉及党和国家方针政策的问题。

☞ 跨文化性
- 世界各国(各地区)的文化传统、风俗民情(folk customs)、禁忌习惯不同,游客的思维方式、价值观念、思想意识各异,这就决定了导游服务工作的跨文化性。

导游服务基本原则

☞ 满足游客合理需求原则
- 以"宾客至上"为主旨
- 认真落实接待计划
- 规范化服务与个性化服务有机结合

☞ 维护游客合法权益 (legitimate rights) 原则
- 旅游自由权
- 旅游服务自主选择权
- 旅游公平交易权
- 旅游服务内容知悉权
- 依约享受旅游服务权
- 人身和财物安全权
- 人格尊严、宗教信仰和民族风俗习惯受尊重权
- 请求救助和保护权
- 求偿权和寻求法律救援权

☞ 经济和社会效益并重原则
- 导游服务既是一种文化传播的社会活动,又是一种可以获取经营收入的经济活动,应注重经济效益和社会效益的共同提高。

小贴士

在接待入境旅游团时,导游应做好哪几方面的工作?

◆ 宣传中国:帮助来自四面八方的境外游客,正确地了解和认识中国,是导游义不容辞的责任。要以积极的姿态,努力将对外宣传寓于导游讲解、日常交谈和游览娱乐中。既要积极主动,又要内外有别;既要因势利导,又要生动自然。

Unit 1 General Introduction to China

- 了解客源国:应了解游客的社会地位、文化水平、风俗民情、宗教信仰、礼节礼貌和有关禁忌等。
- 发挥民间大使的作用:应以高尚的思想品德、渊博的知识、精湛的导游技能、热情的服务态度,为游客提供优质的服务,帮助游客认识中国,增进中国与世界各国人民的了解和友谊。

Discussion & Exercise

Task 1 What are the characteristics of the tour guide's service?

Task 2 How important is the tour guide's job?

Task 3 Complete the following sentences by translating the Chinese in the brackets into English.

1. Tour guides must remain on good terms with suppliers to _____ (保证一切顺利进行) and minimize any problems that occur.
2. Dealing with problems always _____ (需要策略和交际手段). The tour guide should not say "no" directly to any of the guests.
3. A guide must be knowledgeable about his or her city and China in general in order to answer _____ (旅游者的询问).
4. A good tour guide must create _____ (团结协作的精神) within and outside the travel agency.
5. One way a tour guide can ensure that his or her work will be successful is to _____ (尽可能称呼旅游者的姓名).
6. _____ (为旅游者指路) doesn't mean just giving directions to different areas in a tourist spot.
7. Historical and general information is _____ (是一次成功旅游不可或缺的部分), as such details add to its overall success.
8. Guides must always _____ (明白行程中下一项是什么), and pace their commentary accordingly.

Case Study

When touring the Summer Palace, Sophie found the son of a tourist was missing. She quickly decided that she, the dad and two other tourists split up to look for the boy. They kept searching till the park's closing time. Sophie told the group to return to the hotel while she and the father went to the local police to file a missing person report.

Questions
1. If you were Sophie, how would you handle this situation?
2. What measures should a guide take to prevent tourists from getting lost?

1. 多彩中华——56个民族风情画卷
2. 老外看中国
3. 民俗大观——概览

Unit 2　Traditional Festivals

▶▶ 导读

> 传统节日是中华民族悠久历史文化的重要组成部分,其形式多样,内容丰富,积淀了丰富的文化内涵。春节、元宵、清明、端午、七夕、中秋、重阳被视为中国七大传统节日。本单元从起源、传说、民间习俗、社会意义等方面重点介绍春节、端午节和中秋节三个节日。

WARM-UP QUESTIONS

Do you know what occasions the following pictures are about? Do you know their origins? Which one do you like best? Talk about it with your partners.

Text A

The Spring Festival

The Chinese Spring Festival has a long history of nearly four thousand years. Although the meaning and ways in which the Spring Festival is celebrated have changed over, it retains its status as the most important Chinese festival.

The Spring Festival originated in a legend about a certain monster. In ancient times, the Chinese people's ancestors were threatened by a most ferocious beast called "Nian" (year), which lived on various kinds of animals. In winter, when food was scarce, "Nian" would intrude villages to eat human beings and beasts of burden①. People fought against "Nian" for many years and eventually found that the monster was afraid of three things: red color, fire and sound. Therefore, in one winter people hung pieces of red peach wood at the door②, lighted a pile of fire at the gate, beat gongs and drums heavily to make a loud sound, without sleeping throughout the night. When "Nian" saw the red color and fire at every door and heard a thunderous sound, it was frightened and retreated to the mountains. From then on it dare not come out again. To celebrate the great victory, people of every family would paste red paper couplets on the door panels③, light red lanterns, beat gongs and drums, let off fireworks and firecrackers all through the night. Generation after generation the Spring Festival came into being.

In China, New Year's Day is a solemn occasion. Every family performs religious rites at the family altar. ④ This is the time for a family reunion. At midnight following a nice family banquet on the New Year's Eve, the young members of the family would bow and pay their respects to the parents and elders, and the parents and elders will in return give lucky money in red packet symbolizing luck and wealth⑤.

Since the Spring Festival marks the first day of a brand-new year, the first meal is rather important. People from north and south have different sayings about the food they eat on this special day. In Northern China, people usually eat Jiaozi shaped like a crescent moon. Perhaps

Vocabulary

status 地位
originate 起源于
ferocious 凶猛的
scarce 稀少
intrude 侵入,闯入
gong 铜锣
paste 粘贴
panel 镶板
firecracker 爆竹
rite 仪式,典礼

because Southern China has always more rice than any other area, southern people have many more other choices on New Year's Day. In addition to Jiaozi, their most commonly eaten food for the first meal of the Spring Festival are noodles, New Year Cakes and Tangtuan, a kind of round sweet dumplings⑥. Both the cakes and dumplings are made of glutinous rice flour.

A plethora of recreational and artistic activities and events occur during the Spring Festival, including opera and movie performances, lion dances and temple fairs. The dances do not have to be performed by professionals. Sometimes the performers are farmers, street vendors or craftsmen.

glutinous 胶粘的,黏的
plethora 过多,过剩
recreational 消遣的
temple fairs 庙会
vendor 摊贩

Notes

1. "Nian" would intrude the villages to eat human beings and beasts of burden. "年"闯入村庄,吞食人类和家畜。(beasts of burden 是干重活、负重物的家畜)
2. people hung pieces of red peach wood at the door 人们在门旁悬挂起块块红色桃木(传说桃木有辟邪驱魔之效)
3. people of every family would paste red paper couplets on the door panels 每家每户都在门框两侧张贴红色纸对联
4. Every family performs religious rites at the family altar. 每家都要在祖先的供龛前进行宗教仪式。
5. elders will in return give lucky money in red packet symbolizing luck and wealth 长辈则给孩子们用红包包起来的压岁钱,象征好运和财富
6. New Year Cakes and Tangtuan, a kind of round sweet dumplings 年糕和汤团,汤团就是一种球状的甜饺子

Text B

The Dragon Boat Festival

The Dragon Boat Festival is also known as the Double Fifth Day①, whose origin is associated with Qu Yuan, a minister during the Warring States Period② (475 BC—221 BC). Qu Yuan served as minister to the Zhou Emperor. A wise and articulate man, he was loved by the common people. He did much to fight against the rampant corruption that plagued the court, thereby earning the envy and fear of other officials. Therefore, the officials pressured the Emperor to have him removed from service. In exile, he traveled, taught and wrote for several years. Hearing that the Zhou had been defeated by the Qin, he fell into despair and threw himself into the Miluo River. As he was so loved by the people, fishermen rushed out in long boats, beating drums to scare the fish away, and throwing Zongzi into the water to feed fish so that they would not eat Qu Yuan's body.

As the traditional food for the Dragon Boat Festival, Zongzi, is a glutinous rice ball, with a filling, wrapped in corn leaves. The fillings can be eggs, beans, dates, fruits, sweet potato, walnuts, mushrooms, meat, or a combination of them. They are generally steamed. Today you may see Zongzi in different shapes and with a variety of fillings, but the most popular shapes are still triangular and pyramidal and the most popular fillings are dates.

Dragon Boat Races are the most exciting part of the festival, drawing crowds of spectators. Dragon Boats are generally brightly painted and decorated canoes. Ranging anywhere from 40 to 100 feet in length, their heads are shaped like open-mouthed dragons, while the sterns resemble a dragon's scaly tail. Depending on the length, up to 80 rowers can power the boat, with a drummer and flag-catcher standing at the front of the boat③. Before a dragon boat enters competition, it must be "brought to life" by painting the eyes in a

Vocabulary

articulate 口才好的
rampant 猖獗的
corruption 腐败
plague 折磨,烦扰
pressure 强迫
exile 流亡,放逐
walnut 核桃
triangular 三角形的
pyramidal 金字塔形的,
　　锥体的
stern 船尾
resemble 显得像
scaly 由鳞覆盖着的

talisman 护符,辟邪物
fragrant 芳香的
pouch 烟草袋

sacred ceremony ④. Races can have any number of boats competing, with the winner being the first team to grab a flag at the end of the course.

Another aspect of the Double Fifth Day is its timing: at the beginning of summer, when diseases are likely to strike, people also wear talisman to fend off evil spirits. They may hang the picture of Zhong Kui, guardian against evil spirits, on the door of their homes as well. Adults may drink Xiong Huang Wine, and children carry fragrant silk pouches, all of which can prevent evil. It is said that if you can balance a raw egg on its end at exactly noon on the Double Fifth Day, you will be lucky for the rest of the year.⑤

Notes

1. The Dragon Boat Festival is also known as the Double Fifth Day... 龙舟节也被叫做端午节（端午节是每年农历五月初五,因此是双五）。

2. a minister during the Warring States Period 战国时期的大臣（之前的春秋时期是 The Spring and Autumn Period）屈原（公元前340年—前278年）,姓芈,氏屈,名平,字原；战国时期楚国丹阳人,今湖北宜昌市秭归县人。他不仅是一位政治家,同时也是文学家。主要的代表作有《离骚》、《九章》、《九歌》、《天问》。

3. with a drummer and flag-catcher standing at the front of the boat 鼓手和旗手站在船头（在龙舟赛中,每组队员需要鼓手敲鼓、旗手挥旗来振奋士气,同时控制划船的节奏。）

4. it must be "brought to life" by painting the eyes in a sacred ceremony 龙舟必须经过一道"点睛"的神圣程序,象征着赋予该舟以生命

5. It is said that if you can balance a raw egg on its end at exactly noon on the Double Fifth Day, you will be lucky for the rest of the year. 据说,如果能在端午节正午时分将一个生鸡蛋立起来,那么这一年余下的日子就会有好运气。

Text C

The Chinese Moon Festival

The Chinese Moon Festival is on the 15th of the 8th lunar month, around the time of the autumn equinox①. It's also known as the Mid-Autumn Festival and is one of the most important traditional events for the Chinese people.

The Moon Festival is full of legendary stories, one of which is widely known and accepted in China. It can date back to 5,000 years ago. The strong and tyrannical archer Hou Yi, who had saved the earth from the scorching fire of nine suns②, stole the elixir of life from a goddess. However, his beautiful wife Chang Er drank the elixir of life in order to save the people from her husband's tyrannical rule. After drinking it, she found herself floating and flew to the moon. Hou Yi loved his divinely beautiful wife so much that he didn't shoot down the moon. Therefore, the Moon Festival is also very romantic. Lovers enjoy the company of one another during the night and eat delicious moon cakes with some wine while watching the full moon. Even for a couple who can't be together, they can still enjoy the night by watching the moon at the same time to make it as if they were together at that hour.

This day was also considered as a harvest festival since fruits and vegetables and grain harvested by this time and food was abundant. Food offerings were placed on an altar set up in the courtyard. The traditional food of the Moon Festival is the moon cake which is made with sweet fillings of nuts, mashed red beans, lotus-seed paste, or Chinese dates, wrapped in a pastry.③ The round moon cakes symbolize the reunion of families, lovers and friends.

The custom of worshipping the moon can be traced back as far as the ancient Xia and Shang Dynasties. Together with the celebration,

Vocabulary

equinox 春(秋)分
legendary 传奇的
tyrannical 暴虐的
scorch 烧焦,烤焦
elixir 灵丹妙药
divinely 神性的
courtyard 院落
filling 馅料
mash 捣成泥状
lotus-seed 莲子
date 枣
wrap 包裹
symbolize 象征
reunion 团聚

there appear some other customs in different parts of the country, such as burning incense, planting Mid-Autumn trees, lighting lanterns on towers and fire dragon dances④. Whenever the festival is going on, people will look up at the full silver moon, drinking wine to celebrate their happy life or thinking of their relatives and friends far from home, and extending all of their best wishes to them.

Notes

1. around the time of the autumn equinox 大约在每年的秋分前后(每年的9月21日或22日为秋分,正好是中国农历的八月中旬)。
2. Hou Yi, who had saved the earth from the scorching of nine suns... 后羿射日的传说(传说中后羿和嫦娥都是尧时候的人。当时,有十个太阳同时出现在天空,把土地烤焦了,天帝命令善于射箭的后羿下到人间,协助尧解除人民的苦难。后羿带着美丽的妻子嫦娥一起来到人间。后羿成功地射下九个太阳,只留一个在天上。但是后羿的丰功伟绩,却受到了其他天神的妒忌,他们到天帝那里去进谗言,使天帝终于疏远了后羿,最后把他永远贬斥到人间。后羿和妻子嫦娥只好隐居在人间,靠后羿打猎为生。嫦娥奔月的传说版本各不相同。课文B的说法是一种传说,还有一种传说是这样的:后羿觉得对不起受他连累而谪居下凡的妻子,便到西王母那里去求来了长生不死之药,好让他们夫妻二人在世间永远和谐地生活下去。而嫦娥却过不惯清苦的生活,乘后羿不在家的时候,偷吃了全部的长生不死药,奔逃到月亮上了。)
3. The traditional food of the Moon Festival is the moon cake which is made with sweet fillings of nuts, mashed red beans, lotus-seed paste or Chinese dates, wrapped in a pastry. 作为中秋节传统食品,月饼是在面糊中包入果仁、红豆沙、莲蓉或大枣等香甜的馅料制作而成的。
4. burning incense, planting Mid-Autumn trees, lighting lanterns on towers and fire dragon dances 焚香、植树、举办灯会或舞龙

Useful Phrases and Expressions

1. to retain its status as... 保留着……的地位
2. to let off fireworks and firecrackers 燃放烟花爆竹
3. a solemn occasion 庄严的场合
4. a family reunion 家庭聚会
5. street vendors or craftsmen 街头摊贩或手工艺人
6. be full of legendary stories 充满了神话传奇的色彩
7. to fall into despair 陷入绝望

8. to be in different shapes 形状各异
9. to be likely to do 有可能
10. fragrant silk pounch 香囊

Exercises

Part I Listening Practice

Passage 1

American Halloween

goblin 小妖精
squash 压碎,挤扁
stingy 吝啬,小气
beet 甜菜
skeleton 骷髅
jack-o'lantern 南瓜灯笼
turnip 萝卜

Task 1 Listen to the passage carefully and then fill in the blanks with what you hear. The passage will be read only once.

Halloween comes as a celebration connected with ___1___ every October 31, when pumpkins, the most ordinary vegetable ___2___ as symbols of Halloween with black cats, ghosts, goblins and skeletons.

The pumpkin is an orange-colored squash, and orange has become the other traditional ___3___. Carving pumpkins into ___4___ is a Halloween custom also dating back to Ireland. A legend grew up about a man named Jack who was so stingy that he was not allowed into heaven when he died, because he was a ___5___. He couldn't enter hell either because he had played jokes on ___6___. As a result, Jack had to walk the earth with his lantern until ___7___. The Irish people carved scary faces out of turnips, beets or potatoes representing "Jack of the Lantern", or "jack-o' lantern". When the Irish brought their customs to the United States, they carved faces on pumpkins because in

Unit 2 Traditional Festivals

the autumn they were more plentiful than turnips.

Today jack-o'lanterns in the ___8___ on Halloween night let costumed children know that there are ___9___ waiting if they knock and say "___10___!"

Task 2   Listen to the recording again and then answer the following questions.

(1) When do people celebrate Halloween and why is this date significant?
_____

(2) Can you name some symbols of Halloween?
_____

(3) Why did Jack walk the earth after death?
_____

(4) Why were turnips changed into pumpkins?
_____

(5) What do pumpkin lanterns mean to children today?
_____

Passage 2

Peking Opera Course for Children Stirs Debate

controversy 争议   poll 民意测验
grudging 勉强的   portal 门户网站
pilot 试验性的   compulsory 必修的
deem 视为   reservoir 储藏

Task 1   Listen to the passage carefully and then fill in the blanks with what you hear. The passage will be read only once.

China's latest effort to ___1___ traditional culture among its younger generation has raised ___2___ in a nation where diverse opinions and options are gaining a grudging respect.

The country's Ministry of Education announced a _____3_____ to teach students in primary and secondary schools its traditional Peking Opera. Deemed one of the nation's _____4_____, the opera will be added into music courses for _____5_____ schools in ten provinces, municipalities and autonomous regions throughout China. The move immediately drew heated reaction from the public.

In a _____6_____ by China's leading web portal Sina.com, of over 21,000 respondents, only 27 percent believe setting up the course will help promote traditional Chinese culture. Nearly _____7_____ percent think the course should not be _____8_____ as students' choices should be respected, and the remaining 35 percent propose different _____9_____ be taught in different areas since China boasts a huge _____10_____ of local operas.

Task 2 What do you know from the passage about Beijing Opera? Can you tell your partner the different opinions on the above issue?

Part II Oral Practice

Task 1 Group Discussion

Divide the class into small groups and each student will give his/her opinions on how Chinese government should conserve the traditional opera besides adding it into music course? Then report his/her opinions to the class.

Task 2 Role Play

Work in groups of 4 or 5. One of you is a tour guide. The rest are foreign visitors. They came to China to experience the most important festival in China, the Spring Festival, and they are also very curious about other Chinese festivals. The guide is introducing some legends and origins of some festivals in China.

Unit 2 Traditional Festivals

Part III Translation

Task 1 Translate the following words or phrases into English.

(1) 烟花爆竹   (2) 团圆饭
(3) 舞龙舞狮   (4) 灯会灯谜
(5) 去晦气   (6) 剪纸
(7) 年画   (8) 辞旧岁
(9) 敬酒   (10) 拜年

Task 2 Translate the following paragraph into English.

农历九月九是我国传统节日重阳节,已有两千多年的历史。中国政府在1989年将每年的这一天定为老人节,每到这一日,各地都要组织老年人登山秋游,交流感情,锻炼身体。不少家庭的晚辈也会搀扶年老的长辈到郊外活动。重阳节这一天的活动丰富多彩,一般包括出游、登高、赏菊(chrysanthemum blossoms)、插茱萸(cornel)等。

Task 3 Translate the following paragraph into Chinese.

Today, the displaying of lanterns is still a big event on the 15th day of the first lunar month throughout China. People enjoy the brightly lit night. Chengdu in Southwest China's Sichuan Province, for example, holds a lantern fair each year in the Cultural Park. During the Lantern Festival, the park is literally an ocean of lanterns! Many new designs attract countless visitors. The most eye-catching lantern is the Dragon Pole. This is a lantern in the shape of a golden dragon, spiraling up a 27-meter-high pole, spewing fireworks from its mouth. It is quite an impressive sight!

导游服务技能

导游带团技能

☞ 组织技能
- 树立良好的形象
  ◇ 接团前,认真准备;
  ◇ 平时加强自身的审美修养、文化修养、语言修养和艺术修养。
- 把握旅游节奏 (pace)
  ◇ 旅游活动安排,张弛有度;
  ◇ 游览节奏,缓急相宜;
  ◇ 语音、语调、语速适中;
  ◇ 分散与集中相结合。
- 强化游客的集体观念和时间观念
- 处理好旅游者之间关系
  ◇ 身体状况,强与弱的关系;
  ◇ 意见分歧,多数与少数的关系。

☞ 交际技能 (interpersonal skills)
- 尊重游客,热情接待
- 多角度了解游客
  ◇ 从人口统计的角度了解游客心理(不同国家、不同社会阶层、不同性别、不同年龄、不同职业);
  ◇ 从地理环境的角度了解游客心理;
  ◇ 从旅游动机 (motive) 的角度了解游客心理(社会动机、文化动机、身心动机、经济动机);
  ◇ 从个性的角度了解游客心理;
  ◇ 从旅游活动阶段的角度了解游客。
- 发挥旅游团"中心人物"的作用
- 建立合作伙伴关系
- 调节游客情绪,激发游览兴致
- 提供个性化服务

☞ 协作技能 (collaborative skills)
- 与领队的协作
  ◇ 尊重领队的权利
  ◇ 关心领队的生活
  ◇ 支持领队的工作
  ◇ 避免和领队发生正面冲突
- 与其他旅游接待单位的协作
  ◇ 尊重相关接待单位的劳动
  ◇ 及时、有效地沟通
  ◇ 协助做好弥补工作
- 与司机的合作
  ◇ 尊重司机的劳动
  ◇ 做好沟通工作
  ◇ 协助司机做好安全行车工作

导游语言技能

☞ 准确、适中
- 准确
  ◇ 语音正确、清晰
  ◇ 遣词造句准确、简洁
  ◇ 内容有根有据、正确无误
- 适中
  ◇ 音量强弱适度
  ◇ 声调、语调富有节奏感
  ◇ 语速快慢适宜,并做好适当停顿
  ◇ 语感有分寸

☞ 通俗、流畅
- 通俗
  ◇ 口语短句化
  ◇ 避免使用冷僻、晦涩的词语
  ◇ 充分考虑文化差异
- 流畅
  ◇ 明晰交谈、讲解的内容
  ◇ 运用好逻辑思维

实用导游英语

◇ 克服不良口语习惯
☞ 生动、灵活
   • 生动
      ◇ 恰当地运用修辞
      ◇ 适当使用风趣幽默的语言
      ◇ 引用名言、名句
      ◇ 辅以体态语言
   • 灵活
      ◇ 根据游客特征灵活运用语言表达方式
      ◇ 根据不同情况灵活运用语言表达方式

小贴士

导游要做好哪些接团准备工作？

◆ 计划准备：熟知接待计划，关注重点事项。比如旅游团人数、抵离日期、交通工具、游客禁忌等。

◆ 自身状况准备：做好仪容、仪表方面的形象准备；做好面对艰苦复杂工作的心理准备；做好内容和话题的讲解工作。

◆ 物质准备：把出团前的物质准备（接待计划、导游证、导游旗、胸卡、接站牌、门票结算单、交通票据、资金等）写在一张纸或本上，按照提示一一做好准备。

Discussion & Exercise

Task 1　How do you show respect to the foreign tour leader?

Task 2　What should you bear in mind when receiving elderly tourists?

Task 3　Complete the following sentences by translating the Chinese in the brackets into English.

1. It is a _____ (禁忌) to touch the head of a Buddhist.
2. Dealing with the tour escort requires _____ (技巧).
3. You cannot apply _____ (拖延战术) to deal with problems occurring in your tour group.
4. Sometimes the relationship between the local guide and the tour leader can be very

_____ (微妙).

5. Great concern should be given to serve _____ (有残疾的游客).

6. As a tour guide, we must respect the tourists' _____ (宗教信仰).

7. An inexperienced guide may feel nervous when receiving a VIP group, therefore _____ (要精心准备).

8. As a local guide, you shall bear in mind that _____ (正面冲突) with the tour escort must be avoided.

Case Study

Late summer and early autumn are the "golden seasons" for travelers. They are also "action" times for wild animals. Without precaution, people could get attacked and injured. Severe consequences, even death, could occur if the wounded were not treated timely and properly.

Questions

1. How can a tour guide minimize the risk of wasp and scorpion (蝎子) stings and snake bites?
2. How should bite wounds or stings be handled?

1. 宝岛粽香过端午
2. 月圆人喜庆中秋
3. 民俗大观——腰鼓

Unit 3   Local Customs

▶▶ 导读

"百里不同风,千里不同俗。"人们将因自然条件不同而造成的行为规范差异,称为"风";将由社会文化差异所造成的行为规则之不同,称为"俗"。神州广袤,民族众多,各地风俗因地而异。其中哈尔滨的国际冰雕节、蒙古族的那达慕大会和云南傣族的泼水节都各具特色。

WARM-UP QUESTIONS

Can you name some of the most famous local festivals in China? On what festivals can you see the scenes of the following pictures? What customs do you have in your hometown? Tell your partners what you know.

Text A

Ice and Snow Sculpture Festival

The Harbin International Ice and Snow Sculpture Festival is one of the world's four largest ice and snow festivals. It rivals Japan's Sapporo Snow Festival, Canada's Quebec City Winter Carnival, and Norway's Ski Festival.① It has been held annually since 1963. It ceased being held during the "Cultural Revolution", but was resumed in 1985. This is China's original and greatest ice artwork festival, attracting hundreds of thousands of local people and visitors from all over the world.

Geographically, Harbin is located in Northeast China, so its climate is heavily affected by neighboring Siberia's② cold winters. The average temperature in winter is −16.8 degrees Celsius. Harbin lies under ice and snow for as long as four months during the winter. The city's location accounts for its arctic climate, which provides abundant ice and snow. Subsequently, the "Ice City" of Harbin is recognized as the cradle of ice and snow art in China and is famous for its exquisite and artistic ice and snow sculptures. For more than 40 years, Harbin's natural resource of ice and snow has been fully exploited to provide joy and fun for visitors to the city.

Officially the festival starts from January 5th and lasts one month. However, the exhibitions often open earlier and lasts longer, weather permitting③. Ice sculpture decoration ranges from the modern technology of lasers to traditional ice lanterns. The festival has consistently increased in scale over the years, with more talented artists involved and more impressive technology and pieces on show.

Each year a theme is given to the festival, and the sculptures created must fit in with this set theme. For example, 2008 Harbin Ice and Snow Festival set "Ice World, Olympic Dreams" as its theme.

The fanciful ice sculptures are crafted in the shape of animals, plants, buildings, and legendary figures. Many world famous

Vocabulary

Celsius 摄氏
arctic 北极
subsequently 随后
fanciful 充满幻想的，别出心裁的

monuments, including cathedrals, pyramids, the Potala Palace and the Great Wall are meticulously carved out of ice, sometimes in spectacularly giant size. Lots of the sculptures are illuminated from the inside with colorful lights and are especially stunning when seen at night.

With novel changes and immense advancement in techniques, we can now marvel at the various delicate and artistic ice sculptures on display. Today, the Harbin Ice and Snow Festival is not only an exposition of ice and snow art, but also an annual cultural event for international exchange.

cathedral 大教堂
pyramid 金字塔
meticulously 精细地
illuminate 照明
stunning 极为美丽的
novel 新奇的
immense 巨大的
marvel 惊奇
exposition 博览会

Notes

1. The Harbin International Ice and Snow Sculpture Festival is one of the world's four largest ice and snow festivals. It rivals Japan's Sapporo Snow Festival, Canada's Quebec City Winter Carnival, and Norway's Ski Festival. 哈尔滨国际冰雕节与日本的札幌冰雪节、加拿大的魁北克冬季狂欢节、挪威的滑雪节并称世界四大冰雪节。
2. Siberian 西伯利亚
3. weather permitting 如果天气许可的话（这种语法现象称为独立主格，在句中作条件状语）。

Text B

Nadam Fair

There are many Mongolian festivals held every year on the grassland, but the most famous is Nadam Fair[①]. It is a traditional grand meeting and also an annual gala event for the Mongolian people. Nadam means recreation or entertainment in the Mongolian language. It is held every July or August when flowers are in full bloom and sheep and horses are in their best condition[②]. It lasts for several days.

Nadam originated in the early days of the thirteenth century and has been known worldwide for more than 700 years. At that time, a big meeting would be held by leaders of Mongolia every month. Many activities were carried out during the meeting, such as making laws and regulations, appointing and removing officials, and giving prizes and meting out punishments.

Vocabulary
gala 节日，盛会
bloom 开花

Unit 3 Local Customs

Besides, wrestling, horse racing, and archery competitions would also be held. After the Qing Dynasty, Nadam was always held in league every half year. Winners of the three sports would be given horses, camels, sheep, brick tea, and silk as awards.

However, its content and form has changed greatly after the founding of New China. In addition to the traditional sports games, the content was enriched by many new activities, such as theatrical performances, movies, and material exchange. The newly added contents have made the traditional meeting even more joyous, auspicious, and effective.

When Nadam is held, herdsmen wearing brand-new costumes and carrying their yurts converge from all directions on horse or by cart to participate in the fair. As they pitch their yurts on the grassland, people begin to simmer tea and stew meat. All of them are absorbed in a joyous atmosphere.

Wrestling, horse racing, and archery are three basic skills that all Mongolian people must have a good command of. During the Nadam Fair the grassland serves as the natural race court for these fearless people. Colorful flags flutter over the race course and drums are beaten and horns are blown as the races begin.③ Men and women, young and old, can all take part in the race. It is an excellent chance for the Mongolians to demonstrate their superb skills.

During that period, herdsmen often take the opportunity to trade their livestock products for grain and other living essentials④. Since the herdsmen have few chances to get together on this vast grassland, Nadam also functions as a big trade fair for them. Besides farming products, there are also other local special goods provided, such as beef and mutton, fumed food, cheese, cream, milk curd and yogurt. Milk tea and roasted whole sheep are also supplied at the tea booths and restaurants.

The exciting Nadam Fair is appealing not only to Chinese, but also to many Russian visitors as well as other foreign tourists.

Vocabulary

theatrical 戏剧的
herdsman 牧民
brand-new 崭新的
converge 汇聚
cart 手推车
simmer 用文火煮
stew 炖，焖
flutter 飞舞，飘扬
livestock 家畜
fume 用烟熏

Notes

1. Nadam Fair 那达慕大会，是具有鲜明蒙古族特色的活动，每年在阳历七八月举行，是草原上一年一度的传统盛会。

2. when flowers are in full bloom and sheep and horses are in their best condition 当鲜花盛开，马壮羊肥的时候
3. Colorful flags flutter over the race course and drums are beaten and horns are blown as the races begin. 比赛开始时，赛场上彩旗飘扬，鼓号齐鸣。
4. trade their livestock products for grain and other living essentials 用他们的家畜换取粮食和其他生活必需品。trade something for something 意思是"用……换取……"。

Text C

Water Splashing Festival

Being the most important festival of the year for the Dai people in Xishuangbanna, Yunnan Province, the Water Splashing Festival① is said to be aimed at washing away the evil spirits of the old year and welcoming the joy of the new.

The festival usually comes in conjunction with the New Year on the Dai calendar that falls in mid-April.② The first day of the festival is equivalent to the New Year's Eve on the lunar calendar. On that day, every Dai family must clean their houses, prepare food and other necessities for the New Year, and have the New Year Meal. The second day is considered as a surplus day, which belongs to neither the old nor the New Year. On this day, according to the custom, people usually stay at home or go hunting in the mountains.

The third day falls on New Year's Day. People dress in festival clothes, carry clean water to temples to clean the Buddha statue so that they might obtain a blessing. Then Dai people begin to splash water to each other, washing away sickness and other bad things with holy water. They believe that this thorough soaking leads to life-long happiness③, because water is the symbol of holiness, goodness, and purity. It is on this day that the festival reaches its peak.④

During the festival eye-catching activities like dragon-boat rowing, elephant-foot drum and peacock dancing are held. Other activities include throwing embroidered balls, shooting bamboo fireworks⑤,

Vocabulary

splash 泼溅
conjunction 连接
calendar 历书
equivalent 相当于
necessity 必需品
surplus 多余的
soak 浸湿，湿透
holiness 神圣，圣洁
purity 纯净
eye-catching 引人注目的
embroider 刺绣

Unit 3 Local Customs

lighting Kong-ming lanterns⑥, singing and dancing, performing folk operas, going to a fair, and the like.

Although there are quite a lot of legends about the origin of the festival, one of the best known tells of the long-ago days when there was a devil in the village where the Dai people lived, doing all manners of evil. Though people hated him, his magic was too powerful for them to overcome. One day, his seven wives, who had been kidnapped from the village, tricked him into revealing his weaknesses. While he was sleeping, his wives used his hair to cut off his head. But the head began to burn when it touched the ground, and the fire wouldn't die unless one of the women held the head tightly in her arms. So the seven wives took turns holding the head, each for a period of one year. Every year when they changed, people would splash water on the woman who had been holding the head for the past year to wash away the blood and fatigue accumulated from a year of holding the devil's head. As time went by, the ritual became a happy way to send off the old year and greet the new one.

devil 恶魔
kidnap 绑架
reveal 暴露
fatigue 疲劳，疲乏

Notes

1. Water Splashing Festival 泼水节（云南傣族的一个重要传统节日）

2. The festival usually comes in conjunction with the New Year on the Dai calendar that falls in mid-April. 泼水节是傣历新年，相当于公历的四月中旬。

3. They believe that this thorough soaking leads to life-long happiness... 他们认为全身湿透意味着终身幸福……

4. It is on this day that the festival reaches its peak. 正是在这一天泼水节达到高潮。(It is ... that... 是强调句式。)

5. shooting bamboo fireworks 放高升（高升是傣族人民自制的一种烟火，将竹竿底部填以火药和其他配料，置于竹子搭成的高升架上，接上引线，常在夜晚燃放。）

6. lighting Kong-ming lanterns 放孔明灯（放孔明灯也是傣族地区特有的活动。人们以此来纪念古代的圣贤孔明。）

Useful Phrases and Expressions

1. account for 解释……的原因   2. range from... to ... 在……范围内变化

实用导游英语

3. fit in with 与……相符，一致
4. in the shape of ... 以……的形状
5. marvel at 对……感到惊奇
6. on display 陈列着，展览着
7. grand meeting 盛会
8. originate in 起源于，产生于
9. mete out 给予，分配
10. have a good command of 精通
11. trade ... for... 用……换取……
12. function as 充当
13. appeal to 吸引
14. all manner of 各种各样的
15. trick somebody into doing something 诱使某人做某事
16. take turns doing something 轮流做某事

Exercises

Part I Listening Practice

Passage 1

China's Internet Travel Market Expected to Grow by 70%

consolidate 巩固，加强
penetration 渗透
acceleration 加速
trade volume 贸易额
survey 调查
second-tier city 二线城市
industry-wide 全行业的，行业性的
expected growth rate 预期增长率

Task 1 Listen to the passage carefully and then fill in the blanks with what you hear. The passage will be read only once.

The value of China's online travel market is to reach 3.84 billion yuan (519 million US dollars) this year, with an expected growth rate of 70.7 percent, according to a _____1_____ survey.

The survey indicated that China's online travel services market was worth 2.25 billion (300 million US dollars) in 2007, with an _____2_____ 65 percent expansion for the industry from 2006.

Shanghai-based online travel service provider Ctrip.com still held a steady

_____3_____ of the market with the highest penetration in large primary and _____4_____ cities, the survey showed.

"There are two reasons for the _____5_____: the Beijing Olympic Games and the further opening up of the domestic tourism market," said a director of the Data Center of the China Internet (DCCI) research department that conducted the survey.

The effect was _____6_____ industry-wide, benefiting other players such as eLong, China's second-biggest online travel agency, and Mango city.com _____7_____ by the Hong Kong China Travel Services (HKCTS) in 2005.

The survey showed that in two or three years, traditional and online travel _____8_____ will keep consolidating.

The Netguide 2008 survey also forecast the trade _____9_____ would rise to 7.32 billion yuan (989 million US dollars) in 2009.

The survey, begun in January 2007, _____10_____ more than 300 websites, 270 enterprises and 50,786 people around the country.

Task 2 Listen to the recording again and then answer the following questions.

(1) According to a national survey, what has happened to China's online travel service?
_____

(2) What major online travel service providers are mentioned?
_____

(3) Why is the online travel service expanding so much?
_____

(4) What would be possible in the industry in the near future?
_____

(5) Do you like to book travel by Internet? Why or why not?
_____

Passage 2

Rural Tourism Helps Poverty Alleviation in China

> forum 论坛
> portion 份额
> rural tourism 乡村旅游
> underdeveloped region 不发达地区
> shake off 摆脱
> poverty alleviation 扶贫
> attach importance to 重视

Task 1 Listen to the passage carefully and then fill in the blanks with what you hear. The passage will be read only once.

Rural tourism helps poverty alleviation in China, especially in underdeveloped regions with many ethnic minorities and rich ethnic culture.

Tim Bartlett, a _____1_____ with World Tourism Organization, said on the 2006 International Forum on Rural Tourism that rural tourism is helping the country's large rural population shake off poverty while not forcing them to leave homes.

Bartlett said that provinces like Guizhou, home to 17 ethnic minorities, have huge _____2_____ in developing rural tourism. Its remote mountains have prevented the ethnic population from losing their traditions, languages, _____3_____ food and clothing.

More than 200 tourism industry representatives and experts from 16 countries and regions _____4_____ Guiyang Declaration, which encouraged appropriate use of ethnic cultural heritage by promoting the design, production and marketing of tourism products, of _____5_____ handicrafts make up the largest portion.

The declaration also said that while developing tourism in rural areas, equal importance should be _____6_____ to the preservation of unique cultural heritages.

WTO called for Chinese _____7_____ institutions to fund the development of the _____8_____ industry.

Guizhou was chosen as the venue for the forum to _____9_____ China's rural tourism development efforts. It has _____10_____ to promoting its ethnic brand of cultural tourism, its rural diversity and unique scenic spots. Its emerging rural tourism industry has helped many impoverished villages shake off poverty.

Task 2　In your opinion, what is rural tourism? What are the benefits and costs of developing rural tourism?

Part II　Oral Practice

Task 1　Group Discussion

Divide the class into small groups and discuss the prospect of the online travel service. Then one representative from each group will report the summarized ideas to the rest of the class.

Task 2　Role Play

Work in groups of 4 or 5. One of you is a guide. The others are tourists. You are being shown around an exhibition named the "China Local Customs Show". Exchange what you know with your guests while you are watching.

Part III　Translation

Task 1　Translate the following words or phrases into English.

(1) 国际交流　　　　　　　(2) 文化内涵
(3) 蒙古包　　　　　　　　(4) 盛大集会
(5) 祝酒　　　　　　　　　(6) 民间风俗
(7) 表示热烈的欢迎　　　　(8) 尊贵的客人
(9) 主办一系列活动　　　　(10) 不可再生资源

Task 2　Translate the following paragraph into English.

德昂族(the De'ang people)泼水节既是德昂族人民欢度新年的典礼,又是男女青年寻找心上人的好时机。德昂族流行在夜深人静时将竹篮子(bamboo basket)送给自己中意的姑娘以表达自己的爱意。因此,每个姑娘往往能收到好几个竹篮。姑娘究竟钟情于谁要看泼水节那天姑娘背的是谁送她的那只竹篮。

Task 3 Translate the following paragraph into Chinese.

Ice sculpture is a form of sculpture that uses ice as the raw material. Sculpting ice presents a number of difficulties due to the variability and volatility（易挥发性）of the material. Ice must be carefully selected to be suitable for sculpting. The ideal material should be made from pure, clean water for high transparency（透明度）, and have the minimum amount of air bubbles（气泡）.

导游技巧和业务
Professional Tour Guiding Knowledge & Skills

导游讲解技能

导游讲解的基本原则
☞ 以客观实际为依据的原则
☞ 针对性原则
☞ 灵活性原则

常用的导游讲解方法和技巧
☞ 概述法
- 概述法是对景点的景物布局、特色等基本情况进行轮廓性介绍的方法。
- 通常适用于较大的景点游览之前，在入口处示意图前进行的讲解，如故宫太和门侧的"平面布局图"、颐和园东宫门内的"示意图"等。

☞ 类比法 (analogy)
- 类比法是一种以熟喻生，达到触类旁通的讲解方法，即以旅游者熟悉的景物与眼前的景物比较，便于他们理解，从而收到事半功倍的效果。
- 如对法国游客，可将故宫与巴黎凡尔赛宫进行比较，前者在面积上比后者多3万平方米，在建筑年代上早269年；在价值上，将秦始皇陵地宫宝藏与古埃及第十八朝法老图坦卡蒙陵墓的宝藏相比；在人物上，将康熙皇帝与同时代的路易十四、彼得大帝相比等。

☞ 突出重点法
- 突出重点法是指导游讲解中避免事无巨细，面面俱到，而是有主有次，有轻有重，以重点为主的讲解方法。

- 如长城是世界上最宏大的古代人类建筑工程;天安门是世界上面积最大的城市中心广场;长江是世界上第三条大河等。

☞ 虚实结合法
- 虚实结合法是一种将典故、故事、传说等与景物介绍有机结合起来的讲解方法。
- 如游览巫峡十二峰,在介绍神女峰时,穿插有关神女的神话故事。

☞ 设置悬念法
- 设置悬念法是一种在导游讲解中,提出令人感兴趣的话题,但又引而不发,以激起游客的好奇心理,使其产生求答欲望的讲解方法。
- 如游览本溪水洞,介绍了该水洞的地下长河,河水缓缓外流,终年不竭后,可设置一个悬念,请游客猜猜看,这洞里怎么会有这么多水?引起游客兴趣后,导游再说:"待我们游览到源头处时便会自然揭晓。"

☞ 画龙点睛法
- 画龙点睛法是一种用精辟的词语,概括旅游目的地或游览景点突出特征的讲解方法,有助于游客了解和认识其主要特征和精华所在。
- 如介绍云南,她享有众多当之无愧的美誉:"人类的摇篮"、"天然花园"、"少数民族文化艺术的海洋"、"植物王国"、"有色金属王国"等。

小贴士

导游如何做好讲解工作?

◇ 提前查询有关游览项目的资料,根据游客的不同需求,结合讲解方法设好讲解内容和语速;

◇ 介绍景点的概况及参观游览时的有关规定和注意事项等;

◇ 运用各种讲解方法和技巧;

◇ 做好导游讲解工作的"八有":言之有物、言之有理、言之有据、言之有情、言之有趣、言之有礼、言之有喻、言之有神;

◇ 讲解时视游客类型、兴趣、爱好的不同,调整讲解的方式,积极引导游客参观游览;

◇ 结合有关景物或展品宣传环保和文物保护知识,积极解答游客提问。

Discussion & Exercise

Task 1 What are the main presentation techniques that a tour guide is supposed to adopt?

Task 2 Can you give an example of the method of analogy?

Task 3 Complete the following sentences by translating the Chinese in the brackets into English.

1. A tour guide can employ _____ (问答法) to mobilize the listeners' initiative and enliven the atmosphere as well as exchanging ideas with visitors.
2. When introducing a large project, _____ (分段讲解法) can be very helpful.
3. To arouse visitors' interest and deepen their impressions of the place, _____ (重点介绍法) can be very helpful.
4. Sometimes it is also necessary for the guide to _____ (平铺直叙地讲解).
5. You may _____ (进行类比) between the Old Summer Place and the Garden of Versailles.
6. In tour guiding, the tour guide should try to create an artistic conception for the visitors to better enjoy the real beauty of a scene by employing _____ (引人入胜法).
7. The method of pointing the most essential magnificence or importance of a matter is called _____ (画龙点睛).
8. In explanation, the tour guide may occasionally raise provocative questions to arouse visitors' interest, which is called _____ (制造悬念).

Case Study

After getting on the tour bus, Sophie began her introduction on Suzhou's history, geography, specialty dishes, all the way to local customs. However, it seemed that some of the tourists were not at all interested in her presentation, one even going as far as pointing out mistakes in her speech. She felt discouraged.

Questions

1. What are your suggestions for Sophie when the tourists have no interest in her presentation?
2. As a tour guide, what aspects of knowledge should you acquire?

1. 西双版纳泼水节
2. 欢天喜地逛庙会
3. 民俗大观——中国结

Unit 4　Chinese Cuisine

▶▶ 导读

　　中国人的传统饮食习俗是以植物性食料为主。主食为五谷,辅食为蔬菜,外加少量肉食,以热食、熟食为主。中国饮食文化源远流长,普遍承认的有鲁菜、川菜、粤菜和苏菜、闽菜、浙菜、湘菜、徽菜八大菜系。所谓菜系,是指在一定区域内,由于气候、地理、历史、物产及饮食风俗的不同,经过漫长历史演变而形成的一整套自成体系的烹饪技艺和风味。

WARM-UP QUESTIONS

Do you know what the people in the following pictures are doing? What do you like to eat and drink best? Why? Talk about it with your partners.

Text A

Chinese Cuisines

Vocabulary

ingredient (烹调) 原料
nourishment 营养
fertile 肥沃的
prevalence 普遍,盛行
adept 精通的,巧妙的
slice 切片
shallot 大葱
seasoning 调味品
pungent 刺激性的
Sweet and Sour Fish 糖醋鱼
ample 充裕的

Chinese food enjoys a high reputation in the world. "Fashion in Europe, living in America, and eating in China." This sentence is a testament to the popularity of Chinese food around the world. Chinese cookery has evolved over centuries, forming a rich cultural content. It is characterized by fine selection of ingredients, precise processing, particular care to the amount of heat, and substantial nourishment.①

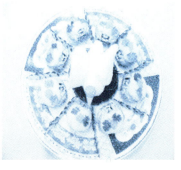

Due to China's diverse climate, products, and customs, food styles and tastes vary from region to region. Generally Chinese food can be roughly grouped according to the country's four major regions: the northern plains, with Shandong cuisine as its representative; the south, famous for the Cantonese cooking; the fertile east, typically known as Jiangsu Cuisine; and the west, renowned for Sichuan cuisine.

Shandong cuisine is generally salty, with a prevalence of light-colored sauces. The dishes feature choice of materials, adept slicing techniques and perfect cooking skills.② Shallots and garlic are frequently used as seasonings, so Shandong dishes taste pungent. Sweet and Sour Fish, one of the typical dishes, are cooked with white sugar and sauce. They are crisp outside but tender inside.

Canton is perhaps the most famous of the food areas. Long, warm, wet days throughout the year create the perfect environment for cultivating almost everything. The coast provides ample seafood. Since the local produce is so abundant and gorgeous, the cooking highlights its freshness, relying less on loud sauces and deep frying③. All the vegetables, poultry, and ingredients have to be fresh. Steaming and stir-frying are more commonly applied to preserve the natural flavor. The timing on the cooking is very crucial. Dishes must not be overcooked, and the texture of the food has to be just right with the freshness and tenderness still remaining. Boiled Chicken Slices, for example, has been enjoying great popularity for its fleshy and tasty meat. A better ingredient is yellow Qingyuan chicken and the cooking temperature is stressed. It is often served with soy sauce or ginger sauce. Soup is essential in Cantonese cuisine. It consists of different ingredients and herbs and is boiled to a rich and tasty soup before it is served.

texture	质地
Boiled Chicken Slices	白条鸡
Tofu Boiled in Chicken Broth	平桥豆腐
crustacean	甲壳动物
chili	干辣椒
eggplant	茄子
exaggeration	夸张
dainty	精美的
esthetics	美学

Jiangsu cuisine, also called Huaiyang cuisine, is popular in the lower reaches of the Yangtze River. Using fish and crustaceans as the main ingredients, it stresses their freshness. Its carving techniques are delicate and well-known. Cooking techniques consist of stewing, braising, roasting and simmering.④ The artistic shape and bright colors add more value to the dishes. One of the specialties in Huaiyang cuisine is Tofu Boiled in Chicken Broth. It is said that Emperor Qianlong(1711—1799) of Qing Dynasty enjoyed it very much and this dish became well-known henceforth.

Sichuan cuisine is characterized by its numerous varieties of delicacies and strong flavors, and is best known for being spicy-hot.⑤ It emphasizes the use of chili, red pepper, and hot oil. It is claimed that it comprises more than 5,000 dishes, of which over 300 are said to be well-known. The most famous Sichuan dishes are hot chili eggplant, twice-cooked pork, Ma Po Tofu, and Kong Pau Chicken.

The characteristic flavors of China's four major cuisines can be summed up in the following expression: "The light southern cuisine, the salty northern cuisine, the sweet eastern cuisine and the spicy western cuisine."⑥ It is no exaggeration to say that Chinese cuisine is dainty, in its items, esthetics, atmosphere, and effects.

Notes

1. It is characterized by fine selection of ingredients, precise processing, particular care to the amount of heat and substantial nourishment. 中国菜的特点是选料考究、制作精细、火候适当、营养丰富。
2. The dishes feature choice of materials, adept slicing techniques and perfect cooking skills. 鲁菜注重选料,精于刀工,善于炊技。
3. the cooking highlights its freshness, relying less on loud sauces and deep frying 粤菜强调新鲜,较少使用刺激的酱料和油炸方法
4. Cooking techniques consist of stewing, braising, roasting and simmering. 烹调术包括炖、焖、烤、煨。
5. Sichuan cuisine is characterized by its numerous varieties of delicacies and strong flavors, and is best

known for being spicy-hot. 川菜的特点是品种多，口味重，以麻辣著称。

6. The characteristic flavors of China's four major cuisines can be summed up in the following expression: "The light southern cuisine, the salty northern cuisine, the sweet eastern cuisine and the spicy western cuisine." 中国四大菜系的口味特点可以用八个字来归纳，即"南淡北咸，东甜西辣"。

Text B

Beijing Roast Duck

When it comes to Beijing cuisine, people will undoubtedly recommend Beijing roast duck. Being a representative of Beijing delicacies, Beijing duck is usually a fixed item on any Beijing tour itinerary.①

The two famous restaurants that serve Beijing Roast Duck are Quanjude Roast Duck Restaurant and Bianyifang Roast Duck Restaurant②, both of which have a history of over 100 years. They represent two different schools of roast duck resulting from the two ways of roasting duck: suspended roasting and stewed roasting③.

At Quanjude a kind of dressing is first spread all over a duck. It is then hooked up in the oven and roasted directly over the flame stoked by the wood of fruit trees such as date, peach and pear, which are used to give the meat its unique fragrance. The best roasted duck is dark-red, shining with oil, but with a crisp skin and tender meat. At Bianyifang, roasting is done in an enclosed oven fueled with crop stalks. Before being put into the oven, a duck is filled with specially made soup to make it possible to roast the duck outside and boil it inside at the same time.

Beijing roast duck is always served in well-cut slices. The chef will show the diners the whole duck first. Then he will slice it into bite-size pieces with both skin and meat. Usually the duck is served together with special pancakes, hollowed sesame bun, green onion and sweet sauce.④ The proper way to eat it is as following: pick up a slice of duck with the help of a pair of chopsticks and dip it into the restaurant's unique sauce. Then lay it on a pancake and add some cucumber slices and shallots. Finally, roll it up before eating it. Other parts of the duck will be served as

Vocabulary

delicacy 美味，佳肴
itinerary 旅行计划
dressing 调味品
hook 钩住
flame 明火
stoke 烧（火）
stalk（植物）茎，杆
hollow 空心的
dip 蘸
cucumber 黄瓜

either cold dishes with its livers, wings, stomach, webs and eggs, or hot dishes with its heart, tongue and kidneys.⑤ The dinner usually ends with a rich cream-colored duck soup made from the bones of the duck.

web 蹼
breed 品种

To prepare the roast duck you have to use a special breed of duck known as Beijing duck. Beijing ducks are called force-fed ducks⑥, which are raised for the sole purpose of making the food. These ducks grow very fast and are big enough to be eaten in two or three months. During the last stage, they are force-fed. A machine is used to stuff food into them every two hours or so. This sort of duck has thin skin and tender meat.

Notes

1. Being a representative of Beijing delicacies, Beijing duck is usually a fixed item on any Beijing tour itinerary. 北京烤鸭作为北京美食的代表，吃烤鸭常常是北京旅行计划的固定节目。
2. Quanjude Roast Duck Restaurant and Bianyifang Roast Duck Restaurant 全聚德烤鸭店和便宜坊烤鸭店
3. suspended roasting and stewed roasting 挂炉烤鸭和闷炉烤鸭
4. Usually the duck is served together with special pancakes, hollowed sesame bun, green onion and sweet sauce. 通常吃烤鸭时还会有薄饼、空心芝麻烧饼、大葱和甜酱。
5. Other parts of the duck will be served as either cold dishes with its livers, wings, webs and eggs, or hot dishes with its heart, tongue and kidneys. 鸭的其他部位则可做成冷盘，如鸭肝、鸭翅、鸭蹼和鸭蛋，也可做成热菜，如鸭心、鸭舌、鸭胗。
6. force-fed ducks 填鸭

Text C

Hot Pot

Hot Pot in China boasts a history of over 1,000 years. It seems to have originated from northern nomadic tribes in Inner Mongolia. Today it is popular in most parts of China and is particularly favored by hearty appetites on a cold winter day.

Vocabulary
Hot Pot 火锅
nomadic tribes 游牧部落
broth 汤

Hot Pot comes with a vast variety of ingredients and soups. Ingredients are cooked by diners themselves in a simmering pot of broth at the center of the dining table. Typical Hot Pot ingredients include thinly sliced meat, vegetables, tofu, mushrooms and seafood though they may vary from region to region. Generally there are three different kinds of flavors for the broth: mild, spicy or Yuanyang style. Yuanyang are Mandarin Ducks who in traditional Chinese culture are believed to be lifelong couples. Here it means there are mild and spicy broths in one pot but they are separated. Diners can choose either one. Traditionally heated over a charcoal fire, the pot is equipped with a funnel in the middle along with a valve for controlling the size of the flame. Today alternatively the pot can be fueled with electric or gas cookers. A combination of thinly sliced meat and vegetables are often served and often the meat is first put into the boiling broth to flavor the broth more quickly. Once they are blanched in the hot pot for a while, they can be fished out and put into a small bowl with a dipping sauce inside. A dipping sauce may include sesame paste, soy sauce, chili oil, fermented red bean curd and pickled flowering chives.

There are plenty of regional variations to this popular form of dining. The main ingredient of Inner Mongolian style[①] Hot Pot is prime mutton or lamb taken from baby sheep raised in Inner Mongolia. Huge platters of thinly sliced frozen curls of mutton or lamb are the main attraction. Donglaishun[②] in Beijing and Little Sheep[③], one branch of Yum! Brands, Inc. now, are popular brands of Inner Mongolian style Hot Pot. The lamb spine Hot Pot, known as Yangxiezi[④], is also another famous variation in the northern parts of China. It is a Hot Pot of stewed lamb spine chunks flavored with spices and herbs. The Sichuan style[⑤] version mainly stresses the sensation on the tongue because people there prefer that the broth is flavored with chili, peppers, other pungent herbs and spices. They believe that spicy food can help keep cold away. Haidilao[⑥] enjoys a good reputation among diners as a Sichuan-style Hot Pot. The southern style or Cantonese style[⑦] tends to be sweeter and features more seafood ingredients.

> Yuanyang 鸳鸯
> sesame paste 芝麻酱
> chili oil 辣椒油
> fermented red bean curd 豆腐乳
> pickled flowering chives 韭菜花

In China, getting together and sitting around a Hot Pot is really an enjoyable time for family members, friends and business partners.

Notes

1. Inner Mongolian style 内蒙古风味
2. Donglaishun 东来顺
3. Little Sheep 小肥羊

4. Yangxiezi 羊蝎子
5. Haidilao 海底捞
6. Sichuan style 四川风味
7. Cantonese style 广东风味

Useful Phrases and Expressions

1. due to 由于
2. vary from...to... 从……到……有所不同
3. be commonly applied to... 常被用于……
4. lower reaches (河流的)下游
5. sum up 总结，概括
6. when it comes to 当谈到……
7. be roasted over the flame 在火上烤
8. roll up 卷起
9. vary from region to region 因地而异
10. be equipped with 配备有……，装有……
11. along with 与……一道，连同……一起

Exercises

Part I Listening Practice

Passage 1

"Red Tourism" Booming in China

boom 迅速发展,兴隆　　renovate 整修,翻修
instill 灌输　　　　　　patriotism 爱国主义
outlying area 边远地区　generate 产生
catalyst 催化剂　　　　Communist Party of China 中国共产党

Unit 4 Chinese Cuisine

Task 1 Listen to the passage carefully and then fill in the blanks with what you hear. The passage will be read only once.

More than 400 million people have taken "Red Tourism" holidays in the last three years in China, bringing in over $15.7 billion to many of the country's most ____1____ regions, according to a state newspaper.

The government has been promoting travel to places connected with the ____2____ of Communist Party of China as a way of instilling patriotism and Communist Party ____3____, and also to stimulate economic growth in the outlying and rural areas where these ____4____ are located and to improve the living standards of local populations. The sites, including Jinggangshan, Yan'an, Xibaipo and Taihang Mountains, are mostly poor areas.

That campaign has proved successful with an estimated 100 billion yuan ____5____ already, a target which was ____6____ to have been hit only in 2010. Almost 2 million people owed their jobs to the scheme, ____7____ directly or indirectly.

"Red Tourism has had considerable ____8____ benefits for former revolutionary areas," A report said. "It has become a catalyst for economic development in many of these places."

The government has also spent 2.15 billion yuan supporting the project, renovating old buildings and ____9____, and built more than 2,400km of ____10____ roads.

Task 2 Listen to the recording again and then answer the following questions.

(1) What is Red Tourism, according to the passage?
_____

(2) Why do you think the state launched the campaign of promoting Red Tourism?
_____

(3) Has the campaign proved to be a success or a failure?
_____

(4) What did the government do to try to push the implementation of the program?

(5) If you are to take a Red Tourism holiday, which place do you prefer to go?

Passage 2

China Approves 132 Outbound Tourist Destinations

approve 批准
destination 目的地
year on year 年同比
mainland tourist 内地游客
outbound tourism 出境游
bilateral relation 双边关系
account for 占（比例）

Task 1 Listen to the passage carefully and then fill in the blanks with what you hear. The passage will be read only once.

Up to now, China has _____1_____ 132 countries and regions as destinations for outbound tourism, with 86 receiving Chinese tourist groups, according to the China National Tourism Administration.

The increase of outbound tourist destinations has played an active ____2____ in promoting the country's ____3____ and multilateral relations with other countries and regions. Statistics show China remains Asia's largest ____4____ of outbound tourism, with 34 million Chinese tourists traveling abroad last year, ____5____ 10 percent year on year.

Insiders say East and South Asia ____6____ for more than half of the country's outbound tourist market, with Japan and Republic of Korea taking up about 30 percent of the total.

Europe, Australia and South America have a market share of around 20 percent. Meanwhile, the United States and China's Taiwan Island, which are considered to have great ____7____ to Chinese mainland tourists, have ____8____ to gain the Approved Destination Status from the mainland authorities.

China will ____9____ expand tourist exchanges with foreign countries, said the ____10____.

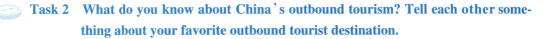

Task 2   What do you know about China's outbound tourism? Tell each other something about your favorite outbound tourist destination.

Part II Oral Practice

Task 1   Group Discussion

Divide the class into small groups and each student will give his/her opinions on the significance of the campaign of Red Tourism in China. Then report his/her opinions to the class.

Task 2   Role Play

Work in groups of 4 or 5. You are having a dinner. One of you is the host. The rest are foreign guests. You are having a chat about the eating customs and the characteristics of various regional dishes in China.

Part III Translation

Task 1   Translate the following words or phrases into English.

(1) 消毒   (2) 大排档
(3) 涮羊肉   (4) 菜系
(5) 正宗清真菜   (6) 宫廷菜
(7) 风味小吃   (8) 打包
(9) 药膳   (10) 招牌菜

Task 2   Translate the following paragraph into English.

许多外国人对筷子很感兴趣，但不知道如何使用。首先把两根筷子拿在右手，用食指、中指及无名指在距筷子近上端处各夹一根筷子，再把拇指和食指合在一起。取食时，把食指和中指夹的一根向上抬，另一根不动，使两根筷子张开。夹取食物时，把食指和中指夹的筷子往下压，夹住食物，抬起筷子进食。

多练习你就觉得它很容易了。

Task 3 Translate the following paragraph into Chinese.

Chinese medicinal diet is not a simple combination of food and Chinese drugs, but a special highly-finished diet made from Chinese drugs, food and condiments under the theoretical guidance of diet preparation based on differentiation of symptoms and signs of traditional Chinese medicine. It has not only the efficiency of medicine but also the delicacy of food, and can be used to prevent and cure diseases, build up one's health and prolong one's life.

Chinese medicinal diet has begun to be accepted by people in the world. In recent years medicinal cans, health-care drinks and medicinal wine made from traditional Chinese medicine have been sold at the international market.

导游技巧和业务
Professional Tour Guiding Knowledge & Skills

旅游者个别要求

个别要求处理的基本原则
☞ "合理而可能"的原则
- 努力满足游客的正当需求 (reasonable demands) 是导游服务的基本原则。

☞ 认真倾听、耐心解释的原则
- 旅游者提出的要求大多数是合情合理的,但导游也有可能遇到旅游者的苛求和挑剔,导游应恰当处理:
  ◇ 要认真倾听、冷静分析;
  ◇ 要耐心解释、实事求是;
  ◇ 要正确处理、合情合理;
  ◇ 要不卑不亢、理明则让;
  ◇ 要不计前嫌、继续服务。

☞ 尊重旅游者、不卑不亢的原则
- 导游要尊重旅游者的人格,热情周到地为其服务,维护其合法权益,满足其合理又可能办到的要求,切忌亲属偏颇、厚此薄彼。

- 遇到无理取闹的游客时,导游始终要沉着冷静。要坚持原则:不伤主人之雅,不损客人之尊,理明则让。

旅游者的个别要求

☞ 餐饮方面的个别要求
- 特殊饮食要求
- 要求换餐
- 要求独立用餐
- 要求提供客房内用餐服务
- 要求自费品尝风味餐
- 要求推迟用餐时间
- 提出增加菜肴和酒水

☞ 住房方面的个别要求
- 要求调换饭店
- 要求调换房间
- 要求住更高标准的客房
- 要求住单间
- 要求购买房中摆设或物品
- 要求延长住店时间

☞ 文娱活动方面的个别要求
- 要求调换计划内的文娱节目
- 要求自费外出观看文娱节目
- 要求前往不健康的娱乐场所

☞ 购物方面的个别要求
- 要求单独外出购物
- 要求退换商品
- 要求购买古玩(antique)或仿古艺术品
- 要求购买中药材
- 要求代为托运

☞ 自由活动方面的个别要求
- 要求全天或某一景点不随团活动
- 到游览点后要求自由活动
- 晚间旅游者要求自由活动

实用导游英语

☞ 中途退团的要求
  - 有正当理由要求中途退团
  - 无正当理由要求中途退团
☞ 延长旅游期限的要求
  - 因伤病要求延长逗留时间
  - 其他原因要求延长逗留时间
☞ 探视亲友或亲友随团活动的要求
☞ 转递物品和信件的个别要求

小贴士

旅游者要求转递物品或信件,导游该如何处理?
- 尤其是贵重物品和重要信件,导游一般应予婉拒;
- 如旅游者确有困难,请示领导同意后接收委托;
- 按规定的手续办理:写委托书,核对物品,办好签收手续;
- 将委托书和收据送交旅行社保管。

Discussion & Exercise

Task 1 How to respond to a tourist's request to extend the travel time?

Task 2 How to decline an impractical request from the tourist?

Task 3 Complete the following sentences by translating the Chinese in the brackets into English.

1. The tour guide shall not allow his/her tourists to do any dangerous things as their additional program such as _____ (蹦极).
2. The guide must refuse the tourists' request to swim in a lake at a tourist site, to prevent any chance of their _____ (溺水).
3. In the event that a tourist wants to change to _____ (海景房), he or she shall pay the extra charge.
4. If the guest would like to give up the dinner arranged by the travel agency, can he or she get _____ (退费)?
5. Some of the tourists' _____ (合理要求) are hard to satisfy.

6. It is not advisable to provide with the tourists some _____ (自选项目).
7. If a tourist wants to buy _____ (文物), the guide must tell him/her Chinese laws and regulations about it.
8. A guide should give special concern to the tourists' _____ (个别要求).

Case Study

Sophie received a group of overseas Chinese. They were not only to travel but also to visit relatives and friends. Some asked Sophie to help get their relatives' contact information. Some requested that their relatives be allowed to join the tour, to which Sophie agreed without her agency's permission.

Questions
1. How should Sophie handle these kinds of requests?
2. If a tourist's relative wishes to join the tour group, what procedure must a guide go through?

拓展视频

1. 京味烤鸭，名不虚传
2. 川府美食，自成大系
3. 民俗大观——中华饮食文化

Unit 5 Tea and Wine

▶▶ 导读

> 作为茶的故乡,中国茶叶种类繁多。饮茶不仅已被证实具有保健功效,而且还是一种闲适和优雅的艺术。中国酒主要分为黄酒和白酒,而白酒是中国最有代表性的酒类。几乎在所有的重要场合中国人都要喝酒以示庆祝。茶与酒已经成为中国饮食文化中不可或缺的重要组成部分。

WARM-UP QUESTIONS

How should we understand the Chinese characters in the first picture? Do you know what the people in the following pictures are doing? Talk about them with your partners.

Unit 5 Tea and Wine

Text A

Tea in China

Vocabulary
Oolong 乌龙茶
minimal 最低的，最小限度的
oxidation 氧化
fermentation 发酵
semi-fermented 半发酵的
efficacy 功效，效力
fully-fermented 充分发酵的

Tea is one of the most widely consumed beverages in the world. As the birthplace of tea, China is renowned for its great varieties of tea which were first used as medicinal drinks.

Based on how it is processed and where it is produced, Chinese tea can be generally divided into six groups: green, black, yellow, white, dark and Oolong of which the most commonly found in the market are green, Oolong red and white.

Green tea undergoes minimal oxidation during processing. It is jade green and has a light fragrance. Representative types are *Longjing, Biluochun, Huangshan Maofeng* and *Xinyang Maojian*[①]. It is believed that China is the world's largest exporter of green tea, supplying 90 percent of the total in the international market. Studies show further evidence of positive health effect from regular green tea drinking.

Black tea, which is known as "red tea" to describe the color of the liquid in Chinese language, requires fermentation; it is dark red and stronger in flavor than the less oxidized green tea. *Qimen Black Tea*[②] in Anhui is the most famous variety.

White tea derives its name from the fine silvery-white hairs on the unopened buds of the tea plant. It is a lightly oxidized tea grown and harvested primarily in Fujian and Zhejiang provinces.

Oolong tea, such as *Tieguanyin* and *Dahongpao*[③], is semi-fermented and has the sweet taste of black tea and the scent of green tea. It is becoming popular among more and more people for its medical efficacy. *Dongding Oolong*[④] from Taiwan and *Wuyiyan* tea[⑤] from Fujian are representatives of oolong tea.

As a type of fully-fermented tea, dark tea (or commonly called "black tea" in Chinese) has been widely known for the popularity of *Pu'er* tea⑥ from Yunnan Province. According to the processing methods, *Pu'er* falls into two distinct categories: the "raw" tea and the "ripened" tea.⑦ They can be compressed into different shapes.

tea sets 茶具
sip 小口喝，缀饮
savor 品尝，欣赏
serene 平静的，详和的

The importance of tea in daily life can be seen from the Chinese saying that "firewood, rice, oil, salt, sauce, vinegar and tea are the seven necessities in every household"⑧. More importantly, tea has had a major influence on the development of Chinese culture. For centuries it has been a custom that a cup of tea should be served to every guest. Now tea, water, tea sets, and the ways of drinking tea have developed into an art form. When taking up a cup of tea, for example, one should first appreciate its color, smell its fragrance, and then sip it slowly and leisurely and savor its taste⑨. A teahouse is regarded as a good place to share ideas with friends while drinking tea alone in a serene room can help rid yourself of fatigue and inspire enthusiasm⑩.

Notes

1. *Longjing, Biluochun, Huangshan Maofeng* and *Xinyang Maojian* 龙井、碧螺春、黄山毛峰、信阳毛尖
2. *Qimen Black Tea* 祁门红茶
3. *Tieguanyin* and *Dahongpao* 铁观音和大红袍
4. *Dongding* Oolong 冻顶乌龙茶
5. *Wuyiyan* tea 武夷岩茶
6. *Pu'er tea* 普洱茶
7. According to the processing methods, *Pu'er* falls into two distinct categories: the "raw" tea and the "ripened" tea. 根据加工方法的不同，普洱茶大致可分为两类：生茶和熟茶。
8. firewood, rice, oil, salt, sauce, vinegar and tea are the seven necessities in every household 柴米油盐酱醋茶，家家生活离不了它
9. one should first appreciate its color, smell its fragrance, and then sip it slowly and leisurely and savor its taste 应先看茶色，再闻茶香，然后再慢慢品尝茶的味道
10. while drinking tea alone in a serene room can help rid yourself of fatigue and inspire enthusiasm 而泡上一壶浓茶，自斟自饮，可以消除疲劳，振奋精神

Text B

Chinese Wine

China has a long history of making and drinking wine. Rich varieties of bronze wine vessels ① excavated show that the wine industry was already well developed by the Shang(c.1600—1046 BC) and Zhou (c.1046 BC—256 BC) dynasties. The invention of the distilling process was a milestone for the Chinese wine industry. In the Song Dynasty (960—1279), using the distilling process the Chinese people were able to make high alcohol grain wine, which is now called liquor.

Chinese wine can be classified into two categories: *rice wine*② and liquor. As one of the world's oldest wines, *rice wine* ("*mijiu*") is unique and traditional. *Rice wine* is a low alcohol wine made from glutinous rice, millet or wheat. After the fermentation process, rice wine has a mild fragrance and is sweet-tasting.③ Because of its bright orange yellow color, it is also called *Yellow Wine*④. With only a 10%—20% alcohol content and its mellow taste, Yellow Wine is one of the most nutritious among Chinese wine. It is also often used for culinary purposes⑤. The better-known and popular yellow wine are *Shaoxing yellow wine* from Zhejiang Province, *Jimo yellow wine* from Shandong and *Chengang yellow wine* from Fujian. ⑥

Vocabulary

excavate 挖掘,发掘
distilling 蒸馏
milestone 里程碑
mellow 柔和的,芳醇的
sorghum 高粱
sweet potato 红薯

Chinese liquor (often known as "*baijiu*" or "*shaojiu*", a strong distilled alcoholic drink) is the most typical wine in China⑦; it has a more complicated production process and can be made from wheat, sorghum, corn or sweet potato. Because of its crystal color, it is called *White Wine*. *White Wine* smells fragrant and has a high alcohol content usually from 35% by volume to 65%. Thus people consider it a hard liquor⑧. To facilitate the slow maturing process, *White Wine* is often stored for 4 to 5 years over which time the full fragrance and flavor develop.⑨ *Maotai*, one of the representatives of sauce-scented Chinese liquor, has become known to the world for the unique climate and vegetation conditions which contribute most to the taste of the drink. *Erguotou,* another famous liquor, enjoys great popularity among people across northern China for its distinctive taste.

sauce-scented 酱香
vegetation 植被
distinctive 有特色的，与众不同的

In ancient times, liquor was believed to tap into courage and inspiration. It was frequently linked with battles in many stories. *Hong Men Feast,* which is referred to as a hazardous plot of killing is one of them.⑩ There are also many accounts related to liquor in literature.

In modern China, people believe that moderate wine drinking is good for health. But as a matter of fact, Chinese wine is so deeply rooted in Chinese culture that it appears in almost every corner of social activities. Birthday parties for seniors, wedding ceremonies, house warming, reunions, and business dinners are the most common occasions on which wine is the main drink to show happiness, respect, and friendship.

Notes

1. bronze wine vessels 青铜酒器
2. *rice wine* 米酒
3. After the fermentation process, *rice wine* has a mild fragrance and is sweet-tasting. 酿造后的米酒味道清醇，馥郁芬芳。
4. *Yellow Wine* 黄酒
5. used for culinary purposes 用于烹调美味佳肴
6. The better-known and popular yellow wine are *Shaoxing yellow wine* from Zhejiang Province, *Jimo yellow wine* from Shandong and *Chengang yellow wine* from Fujian. 比较有名的黄酒有浙江的绍兴黄酒、山东的即墨黄酒、福建的沉缸酒。
7. Chinese liquor ("*baijiu*", also known as "*shaojiu*", a strong distilled alcoholic drink) is the most typical wine in China... 中国的白酒或叫烧酒，是一种酒精度数较高的蒸馏酒。它是中国最具代表性的酒类
8. people consider it a hard liquor 人们称它为烈性酒
9. To facilitate the slow maturing process, *White Wine* is often stored for 4 to 5 years over which time the full fragrance and flavor develop. 白酒一般要窖藏4至5年，以便充分发酵，使其味道更加浓郁。
10. *Hong Men Feast,* which is referred to as a hazardous plot of killing is one of them. 鸿门宴喻指暗藏杀机，就是其中的故事之一。

Text C

Chinese Table Manners

Vocabulary

noticeable 显著的, 值得注意的
pinch 捏, 夹
skewer 串住, 刺穿
vertically 垂直地
ritual 仪式, 惯例
incorporate 包含, 体现
clink 发出叮当声
rim 边, 边缘

Among the many differences between Western and Chinese cultures, table manners rank as one of the most noticeable. Here are some main instructions which may help you get to know how to observe table manners in China.

Food is often shared. Dishes and soup are placed at the center of the dining table and shared by all. Everyone has a place set with an empty saucer, a pair of chopsticks, and often a spoon. When the host takes food from the plates at the center of the table and places it on your own plate, you should take it as a sign of honor and offer thanks.

Respect chopsticks. Chopsticks are the single most important utensil at a Chinese table. As all the dishes are served on "communal plates"①, it is not rude to "double dip"②. You are free to use your chopsticks to grab or pinch food unto your bowl or plate but never to skewer it as you would with a fork.③ Never stick your chopsticks vertically in the rice bowl. It is deemed extremely impolite to the host and seniors present because that reminds them of the "praying to the dead" ritual where joss sticks④ are used which look similar to chopsticks. Lay them over your bowl or plate instead.

Respect seniority. Table manners in China incorporate respect for the elders or the most honored guests. The place of honor, which often faces the dining room door, is for the elders or the most honored guests and the host should sit next to them. At the table, it is the elders who should be first served. Also, if someone raises a toast, make sure that when you clink glasses with someone⑤ older than you that the rim of your glass is lower than the rim of that person's. Understand the language of drinking.

In China, drinking is different from dipping a cup of tea. An old Chinese saying goes "A thousand cups of wine is not too much when bosom friends meet"⑥, which indicates the almost essential role wine plays in the social life of Chinese people. One should never refuse to

perpetuation 永存,不朽

participate in a toast, as that could be interpreted as being impolite. The host usually stands up and holds up his glass while proposing a toast [7] by saying ganbei (cheers or bottoms up). The guests should stand up too to respond to the host's toast proposal. Subsequent toasts can be made throughout the meal from person to person or from group to group. Drinking in China is not only about pleasure, it also has much to do with respect, self-affirmation, friendship and the perpetuation of traditions.

Notes

1. communal plates 公用盘子
2. double dip 二次蘸取
3. You are free to use your chopsticks to grab or pinch food unto your bowl or plate but never to skewer it as you would with a fork. 你可以随意用筷子把食物夹到你自己的碗里或盘里,但别像用叉那样去把它叉起。
4. joss sticks (祭祀用的) 香
5. clink glasses with someone 和某人碰杯
6. A thousand cups of wine is not too much when bosom friends meet 有朋自远方来,不亦乐乎
7. proposing a toast 举杯敬酒,祝酒

Useful Phrases and Expressions

1. be renowned for 因……而著名
2. divide ... into ... 把……分为
3. fall into 属于,分成
4. compress ... into 把……压缩成……
5. contribute to 有助于,促成
6. refer to ... as 把……当成……
7. rank as 把……列为
8. be interpreted as 把……理解为

Unit 5 Tea and Wine

Exercises

Part I Listening Practice

Passage 1

Sydney to Get £330 Million Chinese-themed Amusement Park

> Chinese-themed 以中国为主题的   amusement park 游乐园
> Opera house 歌剧院   replica 复制品
> Wyong Shire (澳大利亚)怀昂郡   model on 模仿
> tap into 开采, 挖掘

Task 1 Listen to the passage carefully and then fill in the blanks with what you hear. The passage will be read only once.

Australia's ____1____ Opera House and ____2____ are set to be joined by a new landmark after a council approved a £330 million, 15-hectare Chinese-themed park including a ____3____ replica of the gates to Beijing's Forbidden City.

The sprawling park, to be built in Wyong Shire, about 50 miles north of Sydney, will also feature a nine-storey temple housing a giant ____4____ and a mini-city modeled on Chinese water towns.

The local mayor, Doug Eaton, said the park, to be finished by 2020, is set to become one of the country's main tourist ____5____ .

"Outside the Opera House and Harbor Bridge, this has the potential to be among the biggest tourist attractions in the state," he said.

"What this proposal will do is turn the Wyong Shire into a ____6____ and bring millions of dollars worth of tourism into the area, which will have a flow-on effect to the entire region's economy."

The council has agreed to sell the land to the Australian Chinese Theme Park Pty Ltd, the private company behind the project. Construction will begin with the building of _____7_____ gates in 2015.

The park will also include a section in the _____8_____ of the Tang and Song dynasties and another in the style of the Ming and Qing dynasties.

It will feature a 1000-seat theatre, restaurants and _____9_____, a royal villa, and a children's section devoted to pandas (which will not have any pandas).

"It is going to be a unique $500 million tourist attraction, employing more than a thousand people and bringing economic _____10_____ to Wyong Shire," said Bruce Zhong, chairman of the ACTP.

The project is designed to help tap into the lucrative Chinese tourist market. More than 400,000 Chinese tourists visit the state of New South Wales each year.

Task 2 Listen to the recording again and then answer the following questions.

(1) What are Australia's iconic buildings?

_____

(2) Where is the amusement park?

_____

(3) What are the features of this park?

_____

(4) What will be the first to be built?

_____

(5) How many Chinese tourists visit New South Wales each year?

_____

Passage 2

798 Art Zone

798 Art Zone 798 艺术区　　Chaoyang District（北京市）朝阳区
Bauhaus（德国）包豪斯建筑
SOHO(small office, home office) 家居办公
cultural and creative industry clusters 文化创意产业聚集区

Task 1　Listen to the passage carefully and then fill in the blanks with what you hear. The passage will be read only once.

798 Art Zone, or Dashanzi Art District, is a part of Dashanzi in the Chaoyang District of Beijing. Now it has become a ____1____ for artists from home and abroad. The area is often called the 798 Art District or Factory 798. It was once one of the several military factory buildings with a functional Bauhaus-influenced design over the more ____2____ Soviet style. In late 1990s the factories were abandoned.

Inspired by SOHO area in New York City, which provided a refuge for artists in the 1960s and 70s, some artists moved to the warehouse ____3____ in 798 in 2000. Cheap rent, quiet surroundings rapidly turned the area into a ____4____ for artists. By the end of 2011, 798 Art Zone was home to over 450 ____5____, ____6____, workshops and organizations engaged in all kinds of activities. Since 2004, many important international art exhibitions, art activities and fashion shows have been held there, which have attracted many worldwide political ____7____, movie stars and social ____8____. Many big international companies like Sony, Motorola, Dior, Omega and BMW etc. have made their promotions there. In 2006, it was ____9____ as one of the cultural and creative industry clusters by Beijing Municipal Government.

The space has become a center of Chinese culture and art as well as a leading international ____10____ for Chinese contemporary art.

Task 2　Do you know some other art attractions in China? Talk about some of their distinctive features with your partners.

Part II Oral Practice

Task 1   Group Discussion

Divide the class into small groups and each student will tell the most important occasions which are celebrated with wine and the different table manners in his/her own hometown. Then report his/her stories to the class.

Task 2   Role Play

Foreign visitors who come across Chinese alcoholic drinks for the first time may be a little wary of them. Work in groups of 4 or 5. You are having a dinner. One of you is the host. The rest are foreign guests. You are talking about the varieties of Chinese wine.

Part III Translation

Task 1   Translate the following words or phrases into English.

(1) 药酒   (2) 酒精度数
(3) 干杯   (4) 烈性酒
(5) 祝酒   (6) 茶具
(7) 品茶   (8) 采摘季节
(9) 提神   (10) 茶马古道

Task 2   Translate the following paragraph into English.

茶文化是中华多民族文化中的一个共同特征。56个民族都有饮茶的习俗。许多中国人在生活中不可一日无茶。无论是在温和潮湿的南方山区，还是在冰天雪地的北方草原，功夫茶、酥油茶、奶茶都是人们特别喜爱的饮品。以茶为题的诗歌、散文、舞蹈、戏剧更为人们所津津乐道。

Task 3　Translate the following paragraph into Chinese.

Unlike Western wines, Chinese wine is distilled from rice, millet（小米）and other grains, as well as herbs and flowers. A wide variety of tonic wines（滋补酒）are made with traditional ingredients. The popular rice-based Yellow Wine is best served warm. It tastes similar to medium-dry sherry and goes well with a wide range of Chinese cuisine, especially during the cool season. Gaoliang and Maotai are fiery, millet-based distillations with an alcoholic content of 70 percent. These are definitely best sampled after a hearty meal.

导游技巧和业务
Professional Tour Guiding Knowledge & Skills

特殊旅游者的接待

导游接待游客时,应遵循"一视同仁"的原则,但有一些"特殊"的旅游者,导游需给予特别的重视和关照。

对儿童的接待

☞ 照顾好儿童的安全
- 儿童活泼好动,又缺乏足够的安全意识和自我约束能力,导游应注意儿童的人身安全,并防止其走失。

☞ 照料好儿童的生活
- 儿童对环境和生活条件的适应力(adaptability)比成年人差,导游在儿童饮食起居方面要特别关照。

☞ 掌握好"四不宜"原则
- 不宜突出儿童而冷落了成年旅游者;
- 不宜给儿童买食物、玩具;
- 不宜单独带旅游者的孩子外出活动;
- 儿童生病,不宜建议家长给其服药,更不能将自己携带的药品给其服用,而应建议家长带孩子去医院治疗。

☞ 注意儿童的收费
- 在订机(车、船)票、游览门票、安排房间、用餐等方面,对儿童的收费有一定的标准,导游要区别对待。

对老年旅游者的接待

☞ 耐心服务
- 尊重、关心老人,耐心解答老人的问题。

☞ 放慢速度
- 考虑老年人的生理特点,导游在游览、讲解、就餐时,要放慢速度。

☞ 预防事故
- 游览线路要选择适合老年人特点的景点,游览时要反复提醒老年人集合的时间、地点,预防走失。

☞ 关注健康
- 安排日程时要保证老年人的健康,劳逸结合,景点选择少而精,以细讲慢看为宜,同时要照顾好老年人的饮食起居。

对残疾旅游者的接待

☞ 尊重
- 导游应端正自己的态度,在任何时间、任何场合,都不应歧视和讥笑他们,也不要打听其残疾的原因,而应对他们表示尊重和友好;
- 在语言上、行动中既维护其自尊心又给予必要的照顾。在提供帮助时注意礼节,如事先征求其同意。

☞ 关心
- 了解游客的疾病特点,并根据其特点事先做好活动计划、生活起居等方面的准备。

对宗教界人士的接待

☞ 学习掌握我国宗教政策 (religion policy)
- 中国不干涉宗教界人士的国际友好交往,但未经允许不得擅自在我国境内传经布道和散发宗教宣传品。

☞ 做好细致准备工作
- 对接待对象的个人背景、宗教教义 (religious doctrine)、教规 (religious rules)、生活习惯和禁忌都要充分了解。

☞ 尊重并满足其特殊需求
- 对宗教人士在生活习惯上的特殊要求和禁忌,导游要设法满足。

☞ 不多加评论
- 避免涉及有关宗教问题的争论,将宗教问题与政治问题分开。

对有特殊身份与地位的旅游者的接待

☞ 注意接待规格
- 不同的身份和地位,在接待时有不同的规格。严格遵守"内外有别"的原则,遵守外事纪律。有问题时,多请示领导。

☞ 做好准备工作
- 做好周详的准备工作,如核实航班、接待规格、用餐标准等事项的落实。

☞ 增强自信
- 导游不要因为对方身份地位高而胆怯不安,调整好心态,提高自信,做好导游工作。

小贴士

◇ 接待儿童团时,导游可酌情讲些童话和小故事,要融知识性和趣味性为一体。同时,应注意一些禁忌,比如:不能摸东南亚国家孩子的头。

◇ 西方文化强调独立,西方人也不愿别人认为自己老。因此,为西方老年人服务、提供帮助时,最好征得其同意。

◇ 来自上层社会的游客,大多严谨持重,喜欢高品味的导游讲解,希望获得高雅的精神享受;一般游客则喜欢不拘形式的交谈,话题广泛,比较关心带有普遍性的社会问题和生活习俗。

◇ 女性游客一般喜欢听带故事情节的导游讲解,喜欢谈论商品和购物方面的话题;男性游客则对时事政治方面的热门话题津津乐道。

Discussion & Exercise

Task 1 What should a local guide pay attention to when he guides a foreign tourist group?

Task 2 What factors affect the tourists' mind-set and how can a guide understand these in order to provide a specific service?

Task 3 Complete the following sentences by translating the Chinese in the brackets into English.

1. Determine their expectations and needs according to their _____ (国籍、职业、年龄、性别和社会地位).
2. Tourists who _____ (受过良好教育的) are usually cautious and expect

more sophisticated services.

3. _____ (老年旅游者) prefer socializing and chattering with the guide while younger tourists are curious about new things and prefer to explore what is around them.

4. Female tourist, especially married, middle-aged women, prefer story-like introductions and are interested in shopping, while male tourists are interested in sports and _____ (时事).

5. On arrival at the tourist site, the guide should ask tourists to remember the number and the exterior characteristics of the coach, _____ (停车地点和发车时间).

6. A tour guide should remind family tourists to _____ (留心自己的小孩). Children are not allowed to enter the swimming pool or beach area unless accompanied by an adult.

7. _____ (女士优先) is regarded as one of the most important etiquette and custom in social activities.

8. To most British and Americans, it is improper to ask about a stranger's age. It is equally improper to ask about the person's _____ (收入、婚姻状况、政治倾向和宗教信仰).

Case Study

Sophie received a French tour group. The members varied in age and physical conditions. They also had a tightly filled schedule. Some tourists fell ill on the second day due to a sudden change in weather. At the end of the trip, everyone was exhausted.

Questions

1. Referring to the above case, what factors should be considered by travel agents when making schedules?
2. Was Sophie partially responsible for the illness of the tourists? If so, how could she have prevented them from getting sick?

拓展视频

1. 茶的故事
2. 酒的传说
3. 民俗大观——茶酒文化

Unit 6　Operas and Acrobatics

▶▶ 导读

　　戏曲是集文学、音乐、舞蹈、美术、武术、杂技及表演艺术综合而成的传统艺术，讲究唱、念、坐、打。杂技艺术在我国已有两千多年的历史，技艺精湛，深受国内外观众的喜爱。其中，京剧、昆曲、吴桥都是蜚声中外，观众耳熟能详。

WARM-UP QUESTIONS

What are the operas and acrobatic performances in the following pictures? Which do you like best? What do you know about Chinese operas and acrobatics? Talk about it with your partners.

Unit 6 Operas and Acrobatics

Text A

Beijing Opera ①

Vocabulary

representative 代表性的
treasure 珍宝
comprehensive 综合性的
instrumental music 器乐
encyclopedia 百科全书
unfolding 演变的
costume 服装
category 种类
statesman 政治家
clown 小丑
make-up 脸谱
symbolic 象征的
loyalty 忠诚

Beijing Opera, the most representative of all Chinese traditional dramatic forms, is widely regarded as a Chinese national treasure. It took shape in the late 18th and early 19th century, when some artists combined the local operas of Anhui and Hubei provinces to begin a new art style. In over 200 years, Beijing Opera has become the most influential opera in China, favored both at home and abroad.

Beijing Opera is a very complex and comprehensive performing art with a unique form of its own. It combines instrumental music, singing, dancing, acting and acrobatics. Full of Chinese cultural elements, Beijing Opera presents to the audience an encyclopedia of  Chinese culture with unfolding stories, beautiful paintings, exquisite costumes, and graceful gestures.②

The character roles in Beijing Opera are divided into four major categories according to the character's sex, age, social status and profession. They are sheng, dan, jing and chou.③ Sheng refers to male leads, while dan refers to female roles. Jing refers to the roles with painted faces. They are usually warriors, heroes, statesmen, or even demons. Chou, also called clown, is a comic character. One of the renowned features of Beijing Opera is the make-up or painted face worn by the performers. It can help the audience to recognize the type of roles, as each pattern or color has some symbolic meaning: red for loyalty; blue and green for cruelty; yellow for cunning; and white for conspiracy.④

Acting in Beijing Opera is not confined to the time or space of the stage. Although the settings are quite simple, usually only a table and two chairs, performers can display all kinds of activities on the stage. Consequently, symbolism is quite important in Beijing Opera. Circling the stage with a whip in hand suggests riding a horse; riding in a carriage is represented by a servant holding flags painted with a wheel; walking in a circle indicates a long journey; four soldiers and four generals represent any army several thousands strong⑤.

In recent years, there is a trend in China for the pop song composers to borrow some elements from Beijing Opera. From this year on, the middle schools in 10 provinces and municipalities will start to teach some of the famous works of Beijing Opera in their music classes. Beijing Opera, the quintessence of Chinese culture, will surely be carried forward in the future.⑥

quintessence 精华

Notes

1. Beijing Opera 京剧，又称京戏，是中国戏曲曲种之一。京剧于19世纪中期，融合了徽剧和汉剧，并吸收了秦腔、昆曲、梆子等艺术形式的优点，在北京形成的。京剧在清朝宫廷内得到了空前的繁荣，被视为中国国粹。著名的京剧演员包括梅兰芳、程砚秋、尚小云、荀慧生等。

2. Full of Chinese cultural elements, Beijing Opera presents to the audience an encyclopedia of Chinese culture with unfolding stories, beautiful paintings, exquisite costumes and graceful gestures. 京剧充分体现了中国文化的各种元素，向观众展现了一部中国文化的百科全书，其中既有层层展开的故事，又有美丽的脸谱，精美的戏服以及优雅的身姿。

3. The character roles in Beijing Opera are divided into four major categories according to the character's sex, age, social status and profession. They are sheng, dan, jing and chou. 根据人物的性别、年龄、社会地位和职业的差别，京剧里的人物可分为四大类，分别为生、旦、净、丑。

4. It can help the audience to recognize the type of roles, as each pattern or color has some symbolic meaning: red for loyalty; blue and green for cruelty; yellow for cunning; and white for conspiracy. 由于每一种图案或颜色都蕴涵着某些象征意义，它（脸谱）能够帮助观众辨认出角色的类型：红色代表忠诚；蓝色和绿色代表残忍；黄色代表狡猾；白色代表奸诈。

5. any army several thousands strong 千军万马

6. Beijing Opera, the quintessence of Chinese culture, will surely be carried forward in the future. 京剧作为中华文化的精华，必将在未来被发扬光大。

Unit 6 Operas and Acrobatics

Text B

Kunqu Opera

Kunqu Opera, or Kunqu, is among the most splendid cultural creations of Chinese people in its long history.① It is one of the oldest extant forms of Chinese opera, with its origin dating back to the end of Yuan Dynasty (the mid-14th century). With Suzhou as its base, it soon became popular throughout the country. Kunqu has been artistically refined over a period of over 200 years and has stood out among the various competing schools of operas in China for its "delicate tunes and elegant melodies"②. In 2001 it was listed by UNESCO as one of the "Masterpieces of the Oral and Intangible Heritage of Humanity"③.

Kunqu Opera embodies the highest artistic achievements that the traditional Chinese drama has ever accomplished and, accordingly, holds a unique position in the history of world culture. Kunqu Opera is a synthesis of poems, music, dance, acting, make-up, costumes, props and sets. Its value is in this comprehensive cultural breadth, with singing as its core.

As almost all the stories in Kunqu are romantic, their performance is definitely full of emotion. As a result, the biggest characteristic of Kunqu performance is its lyricism, where every movement on the stage is in a dancing mode, from the beginning to the end, thus creating a complete scope of performance technique.④ Kunqu dance is divided into two categories: One is mime, used to tell the audience what the performers have sung; the other is lyrical, to describe scenery, the characters' situation and their emotions.

When China entered the modern age, unfortunately, Kunqu underwent a gradual decline from its zenith and finally lost favor among its audience, due to the rapid and dramatic social changes. Yet it has

Vocabulary
extant 现存的
refine 提炼
delicate 精致的
melody 曲调
intangible 无形的
accomplish 实现
synthesis 综合
prop 道具
lyricism 抒情方式
mime 哑剧
lyrical 充满感情的
undergo 遭受
decline 衰落

survived and remained as a highly influential Chinese opera. In fact, other schools of Chinese operas all take Kunqu as their teacher and have benefited a lot from it. Since opening to the outside world, China has entered a period of prosperity and Kunqu gained new momentum in its development. Today Kunqu Opera is acknowledged all over the world for its supreme artistry and it is bound to have an even more brilliant future.⑤

momentum 动力
supreme 极度的

Notes

1. Kunqu Opera, or Kunqu, is among the most splendid cultural creations of Chinese people in its long history. 中国人民在其漫长的历史中创造了光辉灿烂的文化，昆曲便是其中之一。发源于江苏昆山的昆曲，至今已有六百多年的历史，被称为"百戏之祖，百戏之师"。在表现手段上，昆曲糅合了唱、念、做、表、舞蹈及武术等多种形式，对演员的要求颇高。

2. Kunqu has been artistically refined over a period of over 200 years and has stood out among the various competing schools of operas in China for its "delicate tunes and elegant melodies". 昆曲经过两百余年的不断完善，因其"曲调优美而旋律高雅"得以从中国众多戏曲流派当中脱颖而出。

3. Masterpieces of the Oral and Intangible Heritage of Humanity 人类口头遗产和非物质遗产代表作

4. As a result, the biggest characteristic of Kunqu performance is its lyricism, where every movement on the stage is in a dancing mode, from the beginning to the end, thus creating a complete scope of performance technique. 因此，昆曲表演中最大的特色是它的抒情性强，演员在台上的一招一式从始至终都通过舞蹈的方式呈现，从而创造了一整套表演技巧。

5. Today Kunqu Opera is acknowledged all over the world for its supreme artistry and it is bound to have an even more brilliant future. 现在，昆曲因其极高的艺术性享誉全球，昆曲的未来必将更加光明。

Text C

Wuqiao

Chinese circus has a very long history and is an excellent and precious cultural legacy of the Chinese nation. There have been many circus villages in China, with Wuqiao as the most famous one in terms of history, the popularity among people, and the influence both at home and abroad.①

Wuqiao, a county in Hebei Province, is internationally regarded not only as the birthplace of acrobatics in China, but the acrobatic cradle of

Vocabulary
circus 杂技（团）
county 县

Unit 6 Operas and Acrobatics

acrobat 杂技演员
prosper 兴隆
toddler 初学步的孩子
somersault 翻筋斗
trick 戏法
spill 溅出
troupe 剧团
feat 技艺
renaissance 复兴
stunt 特技
spin 转
bend 弯腰
biennial 两年一次的
appreciate 欣赏

the world as well.② Locals claim that their county has been turning out acrobats for more than 2,000 years. Since Yuan Dynasty, when Beijing—the neighbor of Hebei Province—became China's capital, Wuqiao acrobatics began to prosper and became increasingly influential.③ Acrobatic art has a wide mass foundation in Wuqiao, and almost each village has acrobats. It is said that in Wuqiao, everybody from the 99-year-old to the toddlers master some acrobatic skills. When walking on the streets in this county, one may see people take a series of somersaults or performing some tricks just because they feel in mood to do so. When it rains, the children in Wuqiao may run back home with an umbrella on their noses. Some kids can run with a full bottle of vinegar on their little fingers without spilling one drop. It is no wonder that the county has produced many of the most famous acrobats. Wuqiao performers can be found in acrobatic troupes all around China and across the world.

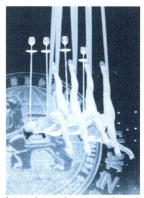

Traditionally, Chinese acrobatics were not shown in theaters. The city of Wuqiao used to be famous for temple fairs which provided a good stage for circus performances and acrobatics. Their performances came from the working people, so the props they used were usually some labor tools or objects from daily life.④ The Horse Feats and the Lion Dances ⑤ were among the most popular performances. After the foundation of the People's Republic of China, the acrobatics of Wuqiao have undergone a renaissance. The techniques have been improved and some new stunts have been added. For example, plate-spinning artists can now spin 12 to 14 plates at the same time, instead of 4 to 6 as before. The performers, usually women, carry out difficult stunts like somersaulting and bending backwards to pick up a flower from the floor with their mouths when spinning plates.

Since 1987, the biennial Wuqiao International Circus Festival⑥ has been held to carry forward the traditional culture of the Chinese people and promote Sino-foreign acrobatic exchange. By now it has developed into one of the three most important acrobatic festivals in the world⑦. While Wuqiao people used to go to every part of the world to make a living with their acrobatic skills, now people all over the world come to Wuqiao to learn and appreciate acrobatic skills, including even some foreigners.

Notes

1. There have been many circus villages in China, with Wuqiao as the most famous one in terms of history, the popularity among people, and the influence both at home and abroad. 中国有许多杂技村,从历史、在人民群众中受欢迎的程度以及在国内外的影响等方面来看,吴桥都是最出名的。

2. Wuqiao, a county in Hebei Province, is internationally regarded not only as the birthplace of acrobatics in China, but the acrobatic cradle of the world as well. 吴桥县隶属于河北省,是国际上公认的中国杂技的诞生地,也是世界杂技的摇篮。

3. Since Yuan Dynasty, when Beijing—the neighbor of Hebei Province—became China's capital, Wuqiao acrobatics began to prosper and became increasingly influential. 从元代开始,北京——与河北省相邻——成为中国的首都,吴桥杂技开始蓬勃发展,变得越来越重要。

4. Their performances came from the working people, so the props they used were usually some labor tools or objects from daily life. 他们的表演来自劳动人民,所以他们用的道具常常是一些日常生活中常见的工具或物品。

5. the Horse Feats and the Lion Dances 马戏和舞狮

6. Wuqiao International Circus Festival 吴桥国际杂技节

7. the three most important acrobatic festivals in the world 世界三大杂技节(包括吴桥国际杂技节、法国"明日"与"未来"杂技节、摩纳哥蒙特卡罗国际马戏节)

Useful Phrases and Expressions

1. be regarded as 被认为
2. at home and abroad 国内外
3. be confined to 被禁闭,被限制
4. carry forward 发扬
5. be bound to 一定要
6. in terms of 从……观点来看
7. wide mass foundation 广泛的群众基础
8. the opening to the outside world 对外开放
9. delicate tunes 曲调优美
10. elegant melodies 旋律高雅

Unit 6 Operas and Acrobatics

Exercises

Part I Listening Practice

Passage 1

Traditional Chinese Opera Big Hit at Latin American Theater Festival

a big hit 很受欢迎的（人、事或物）   wage 进行，从事
Theater Festival 戏剧节   classic 经典著作
ongoing 正在进行的   pilgrimage 朝圣，旅行
Colombian 哥伦比亚人   follower 追随者，拥护者

Task 1 Listen to the passage carefully and then fill in the blanks with what you hear. The passage will be read only once.

Traditional Chinese opera has been a big hit at the ____1____ Latin American Theater Festival, thrilling thousands of Colombians who ____2____ of this Chinese art.

It is a real surprise that "Sparks of the Chinese Opera", ____3____ in the form of Hebei Bangzi Opera, can be so well understood and ____4____ by Colombians, director Luo Jinlin told Xinhua in an interview.

The director said that this time he brought the Chinese opera to the festival, hoping to "help Colombians understand and really enjoy the Hebei Bangzi Opera, one of the oldest types in ____5____, which gathers very important ____6____ of our culture".

"Sparks of the Chinese Opera" groups three traditional Chinese stories, including the popular story about the Monkey waging a war with the Heavenly Emperor, a chapter in the Chinese classic "Pilgrimage to the West".

So far tickets for "Sparks of the Chinese Opera" ____7____ every night during the festival, which ____8____ from 40 countries of the five continents.

The director ____9____ that he would come back to Colombia at every opportunity he gets, because he has found in the country many follower of the Chinese culture who ____10____ and understand the elements in such a way that makes his every visit a unique experience.

Task 2   Listen to the recording again and then answer the following questions.

(1) Is traditional Chinese opera welcomed by audience in Latin American Theater Festival?

(2) What do you know about Hebei Bangzi Opera?

(3) What stories does the director bring to the festival this time?

(4) How difficult is it for people to get tickets?

(5) Why did the director say that he would come back again to Colombia?

Passage 2

Peking Opera Singing Week

feast 节日，盛宴　　　　　　　highlight 突出，使显著
comeback 恢复，复原　　　　　cultivate 培养
practitioner 从业者　　　　　　simultaneous 同时的
Cultural Palace of Nationalities 民族文化宫
Chinese Dramatists Association 中国戏曲家协会

Unit 6 Operas and Acrobatics

Task 1 Listen to the passage carefully and then fill in the blanks with what you hear. The passage will be read only once.

The renowned Peking Opera singing week, or "___1___", will soon offer a feast for Peking Opera lovers in the capital's Cultural Palace of Nationalities.

The week, lasting from ___2___, highlights traditional Peking Opera in performances by singers representative of the elder, middle-aged and younger ___3___ of the art. ___4___ of tickets were sold out as of yesterday.

Peking Opera, the national treasure, is receiving more attention now. Almost all the travel agencies in Beijing have designed some special ___5___ to include a teahouse tour for tourists to experience the fantastic Peking Opera. As foreigners are showing much interest in this ancient dramatic form, ___6___ in English, French and Japanese are now available at the theatre in order to help foreigners to have a better understanding of the shows.

As to the future of Peking Opera, Shang Changrong, the president of the Chinese Dramatists Association said, "Peking Opera is just ___7___, not a decline. What's more, the opera, as an art form, can't be compared to shows that are currently popular, which are only for ___8___." He added, "Traditional opera is making a ___9___ now, and the next ten years will be very important for the development of Peking Opera specifically. We plan to ___10___ people's ability to understand the unique art form so they can fully appreciate it."

Task 2 Do you have any good suggestion for the development of Peking Opera? Discuss it with your partners.

Part II Oral Practice

Task 1 Group Discussion

Not many young people today can really appreciate the beauty of the traditional Peking Opera; they instead prefer to listen to western operas or pop songs. However, many older people are enthusiastic Peking Opera fans. Suppose one student is the parent who is a faithful supporter of Peking Opera, while the other is the child. The two are having a debate as to which art form is better. Try to make your argument convincing. Then report your views to the whole class.

Task 2　Role Play

Work in groups of 4 or 5. One of you is a tour guide. The rest are foreign visitors. You are now sitting in a teahouse in Beijing to enjoy Beijing Opera. Everything on the stage must be quite new to the foreigners. They will keep asking questions as to the content of the opera, the make-up and costume wore by the actors, and the like. The guide must be patient and try to answer all their questions.

Part III　Translation

Task 1　Translate the following words or phrases into English.

(1) 曲调优美　　　　　　　(2) 身姿优雅
(3) 唱腔婉转　　　　　　　(4) 国粹
(5) 眼花缭乱　　　　　　　(6) 精彩纷呈
(7) 美妙绝伦　　　　　　　(8) 翻跟头
(9) 空竹　　　　　　　　　(10) 奇葩

Task 2　Translate the following paragraph into English.

京剧舞台艺术在文学、表演、音乐、唱腔、化妆、脸谱等各个方面，通过无数艺人的长期舞台实践，构成了一套相互制约、相得益彰的格律化和规范化(rules and standards)的程式。它最大范围地超脱了舞台空间和时间的限制，以达到"以形传神，形神兼备"的艺术境界。

Task 3　Translate the following paragraph into Chinese.

Chinese acrobats juggle anything from porcelain vases and glass bottles to people, spin plates on sticks, build enormous towers of people(叠罗汉), and jump through rings of flame. Chinese acrobatics also feature tightrope walking, where acrobats somersault along tight-wires, springboard stunts, and "pole climbing" where acrobats perform stunts whilst balancing on tall poles.

Unit 6 Operas and Acrobatics

导游技巧和业务
Professional Tour Guiding Knowledge & Skills

问题与事故处理

应对突发事件

导游人员在带团期间，必须提高警惕，一旦遇到突发事件，要沉着镇定、处变不惊，要全力以赴、果断行动，迅速、及时、合情、合理、合法地予以处理，尽量让损失和影响降到最低限度。

常见问题与事故

- ☞ 漏接、错接与空接旅游团
- ☞ 入境旅游团人数变更
- ☞ 旅游计划和日程变更
- ☞ 误机(车、船)事故
- ☞ 旅游者证件、行李、钱物遗失
- ☞ 旅游者走失
- ☞ 旅游者受伤、骨折、溺水等意外事故
- ☞ 食物中毒 (food-poisoning)
- ☞ 旅游者患病、死亡
- ☞ 交通事故
- ☞ 治安事故
- ☞ 火灾事故
- ☞ 自然灾害(地震、海啸、飓风、泥石流等)
- ☞ 旅游者的违法行为 (illegal act)、越轨言行

导游应具备的知识与技能

- ☞ 急救知识 (first aid knowledge)
- ☞ 法律知识
- ☞ 组织、疏散游客的能力
- ☞ 应急应变能力

实用导游英语

小贴士

- 入境旅游者在我国境内遭遇事故,若该旅游者是国际救援组织的客户,或受外国保险公司、外国驻华使馆的委托,国际救援组织会直接参与救援服务和善后处理,我国有关方面应为他们提供方便。
- 在我国境内设立办事处的国际救援组织有亚洲急救中心AEA和欧洲急救中心SOS。

Discussion & Exercise

Task 1 How could a guide help the tourist who suffers from carsickness?

Task 2 In case of a fire accident, what steps should a guide take to safely evacuate the site?

Task 3 Complete the following sentences by translating the Chinese in the brackets into English.

1. A tour guide works in an environment where all kinds of _____ (无法预料的事故) can arise.
2. A guide needs to have the ability to handle _____ (紧急情况).
3. As a tour guide, you need to read the _____ (安全手册) that has been designed to give guidelines in event of emergency or other incidents.
4. The guide should also take care of others while you are trying to find _____ (走丢的游客).
5. In 2004, a devastating _____ (海啸) happened in Indian Ocean, which killed many people.
6. All guides can make the difference _____ (在涉及客人安全方面).
7. During the Sydney Olympics Games, organizers were called to take special measures to protect swimmers, sailors and surfers from _____ (鲨鱼的攻击).
8. Warnings about the danger of _____ (泥石流) must be given when visiting an area where rain has lasted for many days.

Unit 6 Operas and Acrobatics

 **Case Study**

Sophie has seen many tourists losing their belongings. Some have lost their wallets, phones, cameras, computers or plane and train tickets. Some even have lost their passports.

Questions
1. How to make sure tourists will not lose their belongings?
2. As a tour guide, what would you do if some tourists lost their belongings?

1. 韵味京剧脸谱
2. "百戏之母"昆曲
3. 民俗大观——吴桥杂技

Unit 7　Architecture

▶▶ 导读

> 由于气候、人文、地质等条件的差异，中国传统建筑各具特色，风格迥异，如南方的干阑式建筑、西北的窑洞建筑、游牧民族的毡包建筑等。本单元将从历史、建筑结构与特色、民风民俗等方面简要介绍"砖木结构"的老北京民居四合院、"大型夯土民居建筑"福建土楼和以"保存明清时期大量古建筑"而驰名的皖南民居。

WARM-UP QUESTIONS

Do you know what the following architectural styles are? Which provinces are they located in? Which one do you like best? Talk about it with your partners.

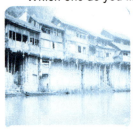

Unit 7 Architecture

Text A

Siheyuan

Vocabulary

quadrangle 四边形
inhospitable 无法居住的
harsh 严酷无情的
patriarchal 家长制的
tenet 信条,教义
hierarchy 等级制度
vermilion 朱红色的
peep 偷看,一瞥
accommodate 提供住宿
adjoin 毗邻

Most urban Chinese traditionally lived in quadrangles called Siheyuan or "four-side enclosed courtyards". The Siheyuan is a typical form of ancient Chinese architecture, especially in the north of China. They are designed to make it as comfortable as possible to live in a climate that is at times inhospitable. For instance, the Siheyuans are enclosed and inward facing to protect them from the harsh winter winds and spring dust storms. Their design also reflects the traditions of China, following the rules of Fengshui and the patriarchal, Confucian tenet of order and hierarchy that were so important to society.①

A small or medium-sized Siheyuan usually has its main, or only entrance gate, painted vermilion. These gates have large copper door rings② and are built at the southeastern corner of the quadrangle with a screen wall③ inside just to prevent outsiders from peeping in. Outside the gate of some large Siheyuans, it is common to find a pair of stone lions to protect the house from evil spirits④. Such a

residence offers space, comfort and quiet privacy. It is also good for security as well as protection against dust and storms. Flowers and other plants are typically grown in the center courtyard, making it into a sort of garden.

It is normal for the four rooms to be positioned along the north-south, east-west axis. The room positioned to the north and facing the south is considered the main house⑤ and would have traditionally accommodated the head of the family. The rooms adjoining the main house are

called "side house"⑥ and were the quarters of the younger generations or less important family members. The room that faces north is known as the "opposite house"⑦ and would generally be where the servants lived, or where the family would gather to relax, eat or study. All the rooms around the courtyard have large windows facing the yard and small windows high up on the back wall facing out onto the street. Some do not even have back windows. Some large compounds have two or more courtyards to house the extended families that were a mark of prosperity in ancient times. Beijing's traditional courtyards still house many of the city's residents within the second ring road, which marks the limits of old Beijing. Siheyuans line the small lanes, or hutongs, that make up most of the central part of the city.

compound 大院
resident 居民

Notes

1. Their design also reflects the traditions of China, following the rules of Fengshui and the patriarchal, Confucian tenants of order and hierarchy that were so important to society. 四合院的建筑理念也体现了中国的传统文化,遵循了风水说、家长制度以及封建社会极其推崇的儒家思想的等级制度。
2. ...painted vermillion.These gates have large copper door rings... ……中国传统文化崇尚朱红色,所以大门的颜色一般被漆成此色,门上安装两个铜环,既起到装饰作用,同时具有叩门的实际用途……
3. a screen wall 影壁
4. a pair of stone lions to protect the house from evil spirits 四合院门口通常安放一对石狮,据说它们可以护院辟邪。
5. main house 面朝南向的房间被称为正房
6. side house 面朝东或西向的房间被称为厢房
7. opposite house 面朝北向的房间被称为倒座房

Text B

Tulou in Fujian Province

The residence for Hakka, the earth towers are well-known with their unique architectural construction, decoration and layout.① These towers are scattered around Yongding and Wuping in Western Fujian and Nanjing, Pinghe and Zhangpu in South-western Fujian.② These buildings were constructed using fire-resistant material and were therefore practically impregnable. The construction material is mainly composed of raw earth, mixed with sand, brown sugar, sweet rice, lime,

Vocabulary
impregnable 固若金汤的
lime 熟石灰

bamboo and wood strips, with the roof covered with tiles.

The Earth Tower of Hakka has a long history. As early as one thousand years ago, some of the original Hakka migrated and settled in the sparsely settled Yongding area. In order to protect themselves against bandits and wild beasts, they used local materials to build tall, multi-storey circular earthen buildings which a whole family or clan could live in. These are the earth towers that we see today.

The earth towers are spacious and they are made up of different shapes such as square, rectangular, semi-circular and round. The ones that are round in shape, which are called "round tower" or "zhai" by Hakka of Yongding, are the most famous and most typical ones.

Most of the round buildings are three stories high with a diameter of 70—80 meters. Its wall is usually around one meter thick. The main entrance door is padded with iron sheet and is locked by two horizontal wood bars. The wooden bars retract into the walls in order to open the door.③ Inside the entrance is a huge central courtyard. All of the rooms' inner windows and doors face and open up to the central courtyard.

Normally, the rooms at the ground level, except the hall and the staircases, are used as kitchens and dining rooms. The rooms on the second floor are used for storage and those on the third level are used as bedrooms. The rooms at each level are identical. In front of each room, there is an open round hallway and usually there are staircases to move from one level to another.

While the round building is fairly large, it has an inner ring, which is like a round building within another building. The round buildings that were built earlier than the 15th century also had another function, that of counter siege.④ It is said that during the Ming Dynasty, Japanese pirates who attacked the coastal areas, always left the Hakka's Earth Buildings alone.

The formation of the earth buildings amplifies the wisdom and creativeness of the ancestors of the Hakka settlers in Yongding County. It is regarded as a miraculous wonder by thousands of experts, scholars and tourists who have been enchanted by its beauty.

Margin vocabulary:
migrate 迁移，移居
bandit 强盗，土匪
circular 圆形的
rectangular 长方形的
pad 装衬垫
horizontal 水平的
retract 缩回，缩入
siege 围困
pirate 海盗
amplify 显示
ancestor 祖先
miraculous 不可思议的

Notes

1. The residence for Hakka, the earth towers are well-known with their unique architectural construction, decoration and layout. 客家人的住宅，土楼以其独树一帜的建筑特征、装饰和布局而闻名遐迩。

2. These towers are scattered around Yongding and Wuping in Western Fujian and Nanjing, Pinghe and Zhangpu in South-western Fujian. 这些土楼分布在闽南的永定和武平地区以及福建西南的南靖、平和和漳浦一带。

3. The wooden bars retract into the walls in order to open the door. 开门时，木栓可以缩进墙内。

4. The round buildings that were built earlier than the 15th century also had another function, that of counter siege. 早于15世纪所建造的圆形房屋还有另外一个功能，即抵御围困的功能。

Text C

Residences of Southern Anhui

Decorated with the typical local style of brick, wood and stone carvings, Anhui-style architecture displays the ornateness and elegancy of the traditional 15th–16th century edifices, boasts historical and research value, while also serves as tourist attractions.

The typical residential houses can be found in Xidi Village and the ox-shaped Hongcun Village.① They have been referred to as the museum of Ming and Qing residential houses in China. Xidi Village is located in the southeastern part of Yixian County where the village streets and lanes have retained their original style for centuries. Hongcun Village was originally laid out in the shape of an ox. Xidi and Hongcun were placed on the list of World Cultural Heritage sites by UNESCO in 2000.

The layout of the individual residences can be reached at Huizhou, where the local houses were originally built by the merchants from Anhui. With their wide distribution and unique designs, the Huizhou local residential houses are considered to be the finest ancient Chinese residences. While Chinese houses have traditionally faced south, these residences face north. They are surrounded by green mountains and blue rivers and each one is connected by a board to the other.② The interiors are a world of natural beauty, where rockeries, pools and flowers abound.

The layout of the houses is very complicated and confusing like a labyrinth. The halls are constructed one after the other, each with a patio to collect the sunshine and to allow a refreshing breeze to pass through. The

Vocabulary

carving 雕刻品
ornateness 富丽堂皇
elegancy 精致优雅
edifice 大厦, 宫殿
merchant 商人
distribution 分布
rockery 假山庭院
labyrinth 曲径, 迷宫
patio 天井
breeze 微风, 和风

Unit 7 Architecture

tier 一层
cornice 檐板,飞檐
flamboyant 醒目的
transgressor 违反者
congeal 使固定

eaves have a two-tiered design, the lower being wider and providing shelter like an umbrella. The cornice is toward the inside, so that the rain can flow to a drain in the patio. The compound is surrounded by a high outer white wall, which can prevent the spread of fire.

The refined sculptures indoors are quite contrary to their outwardly simple and plain appearance. The Huizhou houses contain what are referred to as the "Three Excellences of Huizhou", namely sculptures in wood, brick and stone③. Almost all these houses have peculiar sculptures on their windows, gates and other furnishings. The carvings on the outer gates are extremely flamboyant, so as to show the wealth and status of the family.

Huizhou Local Resident Houses are not only the residences of the people, but also house their ancestral temples. To protect their interest and status, the rich merchants would congregate and form a strict system of regulations and ideas. The ancestral temples were used as the place to punish transgressors and congeal the minds of the whole family.④

Notes

1. The typical residential houses can be found in Xidi Village and the ox-shaped Hongcun Village. 皖南民居以黟县西递、宏村最具代表性。(宏村的结构是一头牛的形状,村西的山为牛头,那里有两棵参天大树貌似牛角,村子南北有四座桥,貌似牛的四肢。而中间的民居排列巧妙,恰似牛的身体。)

2. They are surrounded by green mountains and blue rivers and each one is connected by a board to the other. 房屋建筑在青山绿水间,各间房之间都搭有木板相通。

3. "Three Excellences of Huizhou", namely sculptures in wood, brick and stone 代表徽派民居建筑风格的"三雕"为木雕、石雕、砖雕

4. To protect their interest and status, the rich merchants would congregate and form a strict system of regulations and ideas. The ancestral temples were used as the place to punish transgressors and congeal the minds of the whole family. 为了保护自身的利益和地位不受侵犯,安徽富商还建设了祠堂,建立了一整套严格的家法制度。在祠堂对违反家法者处以惩治,同时统一全家思想。

Useful Phrases and Expressions

1. to reflect the traditions of China 反映了中国的传统
2. to be positioned along 沿……而建

3. a mark of prosperity 富足的象征
4. the second ring road 二环路
5. to be composed of 由……组成
6. to be with a diameter of 直径为
7. the wisdom and creativeness of the ancestors 祖先的智慧和创造力
8. to be referred to as the museum of 被称为……的博物馆
9. to prevent the spread of fire 防止火势蔓延
10. to be contrary to 与……恰好相反

Exercises

Part I Listening Practice

Passage 1

Stronger RMB to Benefit Outbound Chinese Travelers

impact 影响
airfare 机票费用
expenditure 花销，费用
offset 抵消，补偿
retail 零售

noticeable 显而易见的
hospitality 饭店业
soar 上升，增加
stimulate 刺激，激励

Task 1 Listen to the passage carefully and then fill in the blanks with what you hear. The passage will be read only once.

The ____1____ of the Chinese RMB, or the Yuan, should hav a ____2____ impact on Chinese nationals traveling or studying ____3____. However, the impact will be small, and not ____4____ noticeable.

In general, overseas tour costs include airfares, hospitality and____5____. Destination expenditure will be lowered slightly, but this will be offset by the ____6____ in airfares, caused by soaring oil prices. That is to say, although RMB

_____7_____ could lead to lower outbound travel costs, ____8____ tourism costs will not decrease in the near future.

  The appreciation of RMB will definitely stimulate the Hong Kong ____9____. As a popular overseas tour destination for mainland Chinese, Hong Kong will benefit from the RMB appreciation, shopkeepers, hotels and other ____10____ industries believed, "More mainland travelers will come to Hong Kong to spend money, because it's cheaper than before."

Task 2 Listen to the recording again and then answer the following questions.

(1) Who will be the direct beneficiary of the appreciation of RMB?

_____

(2) Will the influence of the appriciation be immediately noticeable? And why or why not?

_____

(3) What effect will the appreciation bring about to Hong Kong?

_____

(4) Why will Hong Kong benefit more than other areas?

_____

(5) What do Hong Kong businessmen believe to happen soon?

_____

Passage 2

Continuing Education Prolongs Life Expectancy

expectancy 期待，期望
gender 性别
mortality 死亡率
obstructive 蓄意阻碍的
obesity 肥胖，臃肿

exclusively 专有的，单独的
disparity 不一致，悬殊
chronic 慢性的
pulmonary 肺部的

实 用 导 游 英 语

Task 1　Listen to the passage carefully and then fill in the blanks with what you hear. The passage will be read only once.

Between the 1980s and 2000, life expectancy increases occurred nearly exclusively among high-education groups, according to a study, which gives ___1___ figures.

The difference in longevity means you would have enough time to complete a bachelor's, master's and ___2___. In 2000, life expectancy for a 25-year-old with a high school ___3___ or less was 50 years. For a person with a ___4___, life expectancy was nearly 57 years.

Life expectancy grew across the board for all ___5___ between 1990 and 2000. But the study is trying to work out why at the same time, the longevity gap between the well-educated and poorly-educated ___6___.

After ruling out income disparities, the study focused on smoking and ___7___. It is found that the diseases contributing most to the growing education gap in mortality include diseases of the heart, lung and other cancers, and chronic obstructive pulmonary disease, all of which share ___8___ as a major risk factor. Beyond the differential change in smoking, there is the national ___9___ toward increased obesity. As with smoking, obesity is more common among the less-educated than among the better-educated. Further, recent research suggests that obesity might contribute to nearly as many ___10___ as tobacco does.

Task 2　How long do you expect of your life expectancy? Tell each other the factors contributing to long life expectancy without looking at the textbook.

Part II　Oral Practice

Task 1　Group Discussion

Divide the class into small groups and each student will give his/her opinions on the fact that people are enjoying a longer life expectancy, and what government should do to help people enjoy their longer life. Then report his/her opinions to the class.

Unit 7 Architecture

Task 2　Role Play

Work in groups of 4 or 5. One of you is a tour guide. The rest are foreign visitors. The group is scheduled to visit Siheyuan of Beijing the next day. They are eager to know something about Siheyuan, especially the history and the culture related to it. They ask the guide many questions and the guide patiently answers these questions.

Part III　Translation

Task 1　Translate the following words or phrases into English.

(1) 多用途建筑　　　　　　(2) 砖木结构
(3) 围墙　　　　　　　　　(4) 雕塑装饰
(5) 通风良好　　　　　　　(6) 落地窗
(7) 拱形建筑　　　　　　　(8) 技艺精湛
(9) 隔音效果　　　　　　　(10) 鲜明对比

Task 2　Translate the following paragraph into English.

客家土楼是东方文明的一颗明珠，是世界上独一无二的神话般的山村民居建筑，是中国古建筑的一朵奇葩，它以历史悠久、风格独特、规模宏大、结构精巧等特点独立于世界民居建筑艺术之林。土楼除具有防卫御敌的奇特作用外，还具有防震、防火、防盗以及通风采光好等特点。由于土墙厚度大，隔热保温，冬暖夏凉。

Task 3　Translate the following paragraph into Chinese.

Architecture and culture are closely related to each other. In a sense, architecture is the carrier of culture. Much Chinese ancient architecture is typically composed of small yards. Instead of pursuing the over-dimensioned architecture seen, for example, in western cathedrals, Chinese ancient people designed housings fitting human dimensions so that they may feel intimate and safe. This idea reflects Chinese culture's emphasis on practical thinking.

实用导游英语

导游技巧和业务
Professional Tour Guiding Knowledge & Skills

投诉处理

旅游投诉产生的原因 (tourist complaint)

☞ 旅游服务部门的原因
- 旅游交通
- 住宿服务
- 餐饮服务

☞ 旅行社方面的原因
- 擅自改变旅游活动日程
- 旅游活动日程安排不当
- 导游工作不力和失误
- 延长购物时间和增加自费项目
- 处理旅游投诉态度消极

☞ 旅游者方面的原因
- 对旅游合同 (travel contract) 的内容理解不当
- 对旅游活动的期望值过高
- 法律意识淡薄

旅游投诉处理技巧

☞ 游客投诉心理分析
- 求尊重的心理
- 求发泄的心理
- 求补偿的心理

☞ 处理投诉原则
- 耐心倾听,不与争辩
- 表示同情和理解,不盲目做出承诺
- 调查了解,迅速答复
- 事后总结,记录存档 (keep in the archives)

Unit 7 Architecture

> **小贴士**
>
> **旅游消费维权方式有哪些?**
> ◆ 与旅游经营者协商和解;
> ◆ 请求消费者协会调解;
> ◆ 向有关行政部门申诉;
> ◆ 根据与经营者达成的仲裁协议,提请仲裁机构仲裁;
> ◆ 向人民法院提起诉讼。

Discussion & Exercise

Task 1   What kind of activities may result in tourists' complaints?

Task 2   What kind of compensation can be provided when dealing with these complaints?

Task 3   Complete the following sentences by translating the Chinese in the brackets into English.

1. I'd like to _____ (投诉) about my holiday in Thailand last week.
2. This insurance company cannot meet such enormous _____ (索赔).
3. Because your agency caused the problems, we expect you to work with us to get a _____ (满意的结果).
4. If you don't solve the problem for me, I'll report you to the appropriate _____ (职能管理部门).
5. I will _____ (调查此事) at once.
6. You must apologize rather than only say "sorry" for _____ (不便) you caused us.
7. I will _____ (处理此事) right away.
8. Please accept our _____ (真诚的道歉) for any inconvenience.

Case Study

In the middle of a tour, a tourist complained to Sophie about her service. He said that his family should not have been put in upper berths, in separate rooms, and that the tour presentation was on the whole perfunctory (敷衍的, 马虎的). He demanded a refund and requested to cancel the tour midway. Otherwise he would complain to Sophie's superiors.

Questions
1. How should Sophie handle the tourist's complaints?
2. What might be some of the reasons for quitting the tour midway? How does a guide handle this?

1. 四合院内大天地
2. 土楼神韵
3. 民俗大观——民居文化

Unit 8　Religion

▶▶ 导读

> 中国是个多宗教的国家,现有各种宗教信徒一亿多人。具有一定历史影响、形成中华民族风范、拥有一定规模性和区域性的信教教别主要有佛教、道教、伊斯兰教、天主教和基督教,它们被称为"中国五大宗教"。在我国,各种宗教地位平等,和谐共处,宗教信仰自由受到法律保护。

WARM-UP QUESTIONS

Do you know what are illustrated in the following pictures? What religion does each picture represent? Do you know something about the religions in the world? Talk about them with your partners.

Text A

Buddhism

Vocabulary

enlighten 启发,顿悟
impermanent 非永久性的
adherent 信徒
simplicity 简单,朴素
foothold 立足点
Chan/Zen 禅
salvation 救赎
shift 转变
exposition 解释,阐述

Buddhism is one of the world's great religions and originated in 563 BC in India. It derives from the teaching of the Buddha[①], who is regarded as one of a series of such enlightened beings. The person who believes in Buddha is called a Buddhist.

Buddhists believe that all beings (including gods) are impermanent, unsatisfactory and lack a permanent essence.[②] In the first place everything in life is constantly changing and impermanent. In the second place, everything is unsatisfactory in life because everything is impermanent. Finally, there is no eternal soul.

Buddhism entered China a few centuries after Buddha passed away, at the time when Confucianism and Taoism were the dominant religions[③]. At first, Buddhism did not find many adherents in China. But by the 2nd Century AD, aided, to some extent, by the simplicity of its approach and some similarities with Taoism, it managed to gain a firm foothold and acquired a sizeable following.[④]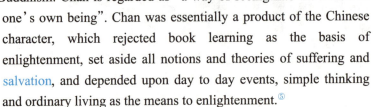

The most popular school of the Chinese Buddhism is Chan, which became popular in Japan and later in the west as Zen Buddhism. Chan is regarded as "a way of seeing into the nature of one's own being". Chan was essentially a product of the Chinese character, which rejected book learning as the basis of enlightenment, set aside all notions and theories of suffering and salvation, and depended upon day to day events, simple thinking and ordinary living as the means to enlightenment.[⑤]

For Chan School, enlightenment descended upon one as a sudden shift in awareness, not because of any elaborate study of the Buddhist sutras, exposition of the philosophies, nor worship of the images of Buddha.[⑥]

However, the Chan School discouraged the intellectual kind

of pursuit of religion because it believed that any scholarly approach would tend to stiffen the mind and prevent it from experiencing the sudden flowering of Chan⑦.

scholarly 学术的
stiffen 使僵硬
spontaneity 自发，自主

It is an evident fact that Chan Buddhism had a profound effect on the Chinese way of life. Meanwhile, the Chan art became famous and flourished in ancient China, due to its spontaneity and simplicity of expression.⑧ But with the decline of Buddhism in China, Chan also gradually retreated into remote monasteries and gradually lost its appeal.

Notes

1. teaching of the Buddha 佛祖的教义

2. Buddhists believe that all beings (including gods) are impermanent, unsatisfactory and lack a permanent essence. 佛教徒认为众生（包括佛祖）都不是永恒不变的，都是不能完全感到满足的，他们没有一个永恒不变的灵魂。

3. at a time when Confucianism and Taoism were the dominant religions 在儒家思想和道家思想占统治地位的时候

4. it managed to gain a firm foothold and acquired a sizeable following （佛教）终于立住脚跟并拥有一定数量的追随者

5. Chan was essentially a product of Chinese character, which rejected book learning as the basis of enlightenment, set aside all notions and theories of suffering and salvation, and depended upon day to day events, simple thinking and ordinary living as the means to enlightenment. 禅在本质上是中国特色的产物。禅抛弃将经书的阅读作为觉悟的方式，并且置苦难和救赎理论于一旁，而完全依靠每日繁琐事件、朴素的思想和日常生活作为觉悟的方式。

6. For Chan School, enlightenment descended upon one as a sudden shift in awareness, not because of any elaborate study of the Buddhist sutras, exposition of the philosophies, nor worship of the images of the Buddha. 对于禅学而言，觉悟是意识的突然转变，而不是因为对佛经的仔细研读、对哲学思想的阐释或是对佛像的崇拜。

7. any scholarly approach would tend to stiffen the mind and prevent it from experiencing the sudden flowering of Chan 任何学术方法都会使思想僵硬，从而无法体验禅的觉悟

8. Meanwhile, the Chan art became famous and flourished in ancient China, due to its spontaneity and simplicity of expression. 同时，禅学艺术因其自觉性与表达的朴素性在古代中国非常繁荣。

Text B

Taoism

Taoism is a genuinely Chinese religion and can help one gain a much better understanding of Chinese culture. The creator of Taoism is Lao Zi who was a renowned thinker around 6th century BC. The ideological system of Taoism covers a wide range of contents.① Tao is the origin of the eternal world. It is boundless in time and space. Generally speaking, it evolved into a religious culture by basing itself on ancient religious beliefs in China, including the worship of heaven and ancestors, as well as Taoist theories and beliefs regarding immortality.② It has also absorbed ethical ideas from Confucianism and folk religious customs.

According to Taoism, ordinary people can become gods when they have Dao. Taoism pursues immortality and preservation of health whose uttermost goal is to become an immortal being.③ Taoism claims this can be obtained through cultivating one's moral character and perfecting one's moral integrity.

The core of Taoism is "Dao"④. It is said that "Dao" is the origin of the universe, the basis of all existing things, the law governing their development and change, and the ultimate god of Taoism.⑤ The concept of Virtue (De) is closely related to Dao. The highest ideal of a Taoist is to acquire immortality. To achieve this goal, one must practice Taoism both inside and outside of one's physical existence. Inner practice involves physical and breathing exercises, concentrated contemplation and the taking of elixirs.⑥ Later, this type of practice gradually came down to refining the interior elixirs (neidan).⑦

The basic principle of this practice is still to cultivate the self both spiritually and physically. External practice involves doing good deeds and helping others so as to acquire more merits and virtues. If one succeeds in both aspects, one could enter the world of immortals.

Vocabulary

genuinely 真正的
ideological 思想的
absorb 吸收
preservation 保存
integrity 正直,诚实
ultimate 最终的
concept 概念
contemplation 冥想
interior 内在的

Taoism has also found its way to other parts of the world. Taoist methods of keeping fit and healthy, as well as the Taoist concept of harmonious coexistence between humans and nature, have claimed a great deal of attention⑧.

Taoism is attracting the interest of an increasing number of people worldwide. The emblem of Taoism is the Taiji symbol, or diagram of the cosmological scheme, comprised of a circle with an S-shaped line dividing the white (Yang) and black (Yin) halves.

> harmonious 和谐的
> coexistence 共存
> emblem 象征,符号
> cosmological 宇宙的
> halve 相对等的两部分

Notes

1. The ideological system of Taoism covers a wide range of contents. 道教的思想体系包含很多内容。

2. Generally speaking, it evolved into a religious culture by basing itself on ancient religious beliefs in China, including the worship of heaven and ancestors, as well as Taoist theories and beliefs regarding immortality. 总体而言,道教之所以能够发展成为一种宗教文化,其根本原因在于道教思想是建立在古代中国对于天地和祖先的崇拜的宗教信仰以及关于长生的道教理论和信仰的基础之上的。

3. According to Taoism, ordinary people can become gods when they have Dao. Taoism pursues immortality and preservation of health whose uttermost goal is to become an immortal being. 根据道家思想,寻常百姓只要得道便能成仙。道教所追求的是长生不老,而其最终目的也是长生不死。

4. The core of Taoism is "Dao". 道教的核心思想是"道"。

5. It is said that "Dao" is the origin of the universe, the basis of all existing things, the law governing their development and change, and the ultimate god of Taoism. 据说,"道"是宇宙的源头,是万物之本,是掌控万物发展与变化的规律,也是道教思想的最高神明。

6. Inner practice involves physical and breathing exercises, concentrated contemplation and the taking of elixirs. 内练包括身体锻炼、呼吸训练、冥想以及服用仙丹。

7. Later, this type of practice gradually came down to refining the interior elixirs (neidan). 后来,此类的练习逐渐被称为内练(内丹)。

8. as well as the Taoist concept of harmonious coexistence between humans and nature, have claimed a great deal of attention 同时,道教思想所倡导的人与自然的和谐共存也引起了许多关注

实用导游英语

Text C

Islam

Vocabulary
Muslim 伊斯兰信徒
Prophet 先知
Nazareth 拿撒勒（巴勒斯坦北部古城）
glare 强光，闪耀
formalize 使正式，使定形
clarify 使清楚
purify 净化
besiege 围攻
virtually 实际上
dominate 主宰，掌控

Islam, whose name is derived from the Arabic word "salam", is often interpreted as meaning "peace". The followers of Islam are called Muslims. "Allah" is an Arabic word which means "the One True God". Most religious historians view Islam as being founded in 622 by Muhammad the Prophet. Different from other great religious leaders, such as the Buddha, Moses and Yeshua of Nazareth (Jesus Christ), Muhammad was born relatively recently, in the late 6th century, about the year 570.① It is said that Muhammad was probably the first religious leader to rise up in the full glare of history.

However, many researchers do not look upon Islam as a new religion. They feel that it is in reality the faith taught by the ancient Prophets: Abraham, David, Moses and Jesus. Muhammad's role as the last of the Prophets was to formalize and clarify the faith and to purify it by removing foreign ideas that had been wrongly added to it.②

By 750, Islam had come to China, India, the Southern shore of the Mediterranean and Spain. In 1550, Islamic military forces had besieged Vienna. Since their trading routes were mostly over land, they did not develop extensive maritime commerce. As a result, the old world occupation of North America was left to Christians.③ Believers of Islam are presently concentrated in the areas from the West coast of Africa to the Philippines④. In particular, in Africa, these believers are increasing in numbers, largely at the expense of Christianity.⑤

It is believed that Muslims, since the seventh century, have managed to practise their faith in China, sometimes against great odds⑥. Many Muslims went to China to trade, and these Muslims began to have a great economic impact and influence on the country. Muslims virtually dominated the import and export industry by the time of the Song Dynasty (960—1279).

At present, Islam is one of the religions that are officially

Unit 8 Religion

recognized in China. Under China's current leadership, Islam is undergoing a modest revival and there are now many mosques in China. There has been an upsurge in Islamic expression and many nation-wide Islamic associations have been organized to coordinate inter-ethnic activities among Muslims.

revival 复兴
upsurge 高涨
inter-ethnic 种族之间的
repertoire 所有组成部分
monotheism 一神论
Koran《古兰经》

Over the centuries, the Islamic experience has provided an abundant repertoire. All Muslims continued to affirm the basic core of the faith in monotheism as defined by the revelation to Muhammad and preserved in the *Koran*.⑦

Notes

1. Different from the other great religious leaders, such as the Buddha, Moses and Yeshua of Nazareth (Jesus Christ), Muhammad was born relatively recently, in the late 6th century, about the year 570. 与其他的宗教创始人诸如释迦牟尼、摩西和拿撒勒的耶和华(耶稣基督)不同，穆罕默德出生相对较晚，大概是公元6世纪，约570年。

2. Muhammad's role as the last of the Prophets was to formalize and clarify the faith and to purify it by removing foreign ideas that had been wrongly added to it. 穆罕默德作为最后一位先知的作用在于通过排除因错而添加的异教思想从而规范和澄清信仰使之纯净。

3. As a result, the old world occupation of North America was left to Christians. 因此，北美大陆就只能留给基督教徒了。

4. believers of Islam are presently concentrated in the areas from the West coast of Africa to the Philippines 现在，穆斯林信徒主要集中在非洲的西海岸到菲律宾群岛

5. In particular, in Africa, these believers are increasing in numbers, largely at the expense of Christianity. 尤其在非洲，穆斯林信徒数目大量增加，而基督教信徒的数目则大量减少。

6. sometimes against geat odds 有时需要克服巨大困难

7. All Muslims continued to affirm the basic core of the faith in monotheism as defined by the revelation to Muhammad and preserved in the *Koran*. 所有的穆斯林信徒一直坚信穆罕默德所揭示的和《古兰经》所保存的一神论的基本准则。

Useful Phrases and Expressions

1. pass away 过世
2. gain a firm foothold 站住脚跟
3. set aside 摈弃，置之一旁
4. a wide range of 大量的
5. claim a great deal of attention 引起大量注意

6. be compromised of 由……构成
7. derive from 来源于
8. rise up in the full glare of the history 点亮了历史的闪耀之光
9. an upsurge in Islamic expression 穆斯林思想的高涨

Exercises

Part I Listening Practice

Passage 1

The Differences between Christianity and Buddhism

Christianity 基督教
have little in common 很不相同
similar to 与……相似
at first glance 第一眼
cease 停止
by contrast 相反

Task 1 Listen to the passage carefully and then fill in the blanks with what you hear. The passage will be read only once.

When talking about the differences between Buddhism and Christianity, it is difficult to know where to start because there are so many _____1_____ to cover. Buddhism and Christianity are different from each other in most of their _____2_____, though not quite as much as one might think, at first glance.

Now, those who believe in an afterlife believe that it won't be like the life that we _____3_____ have, but a surprising number of belief systems hold that the afterlife is mostly like this one, only _____4_____. Now, both Christianity and Buddhism hold that there is a life after this one. However, the exact _____5_____ of that afterlife has little in common with at least some _____6_____. For the ones that _____7_____ believe in enlightenment as ceasing to exist, this differs very obviously from Christianity because Christianity holds that people will continue to exist after death.

Even with Buddhism which does believe in ____8____ after enlightenment, Christianity has much more of an emphasis on personal existence. Even in the Buddhism which is most similar to Christianity, personal existence is not a ____9____ thing; it is a thing to be overcome. Christianity, by contrast, ____10____ personal existence and almost indulges in it.

Task 2   Listen to the recording again and then answer the following questions.

(1) Why is it difficult to start elaborating on the differences between Christianity and Buddhism?

_____

(2) What might one think about the difference between Christianity and Buddhism at first glance?

_____

(3) What is the afterlife like according to most people?

_____

(4) What does afterlife mean to Buddhism believers?

_____

(5) What does the Christianity put emphasis on according to the passage?

_____

Passage 2

The Differences between Buddhism and Taoism

doctrinal 条例的，学说的
exert a deep influence on 产生影响
Celestial Master 天师
Sanskrit 梵语

实 用 导 游 英 语

Task 1 Listen to the passage carefully and then fill in the blanks with what you hear. The passage will be read only once.

It is an inevitable fact that Taoism differs quite _____1_____ from Buddhism due to the doctrinal differences between Buddhism and Taoism, which might cause _____2_____ in various aspects.

Buddhism, as a foreign culture, came to China and underwent mainly three stages of the development in China until it's being a major religion in China. This process of development can be referred to as _____3_____ to a certain extent. Taoism, as an indigenous traditional religion of China, is generally believed that Taoist organizations were formally _____4_____ 1,900 years ago by Celestial Master Zhang Daoling during the reign (126-144) of Emperor Shundi of the Eastern Han Dynasty.

However, in history, the Buddhist monks and Taoists had always argued about the _____5_____ of each own religion so as to fight for a higher position in the society politically. Buddhism had exerted a deep influence on the Chinese _____6_____. The process of translation of the Buddhist scriptures from Sanskrit into Chinese had given impetus to a new development of the Chinese poem, _____7_____ and novel. Meanwhile, Taoism, during its time-honored history of development, has also brought far-reaching influence on China's philosophy, literature, arts, medicine and science. What _____8_____ special attention is its great contribution to ancient Chinese medicinal _____9_____.

Now, China has been a place where Confucianism, Buddhism and Taoism, the three major _____10_____ schools flowed together taking on a new aspect in the Chinese society.

Task 2 Have you got a clear idea of the main religions in China? Tell each other the differences between Buddhism, Taoism and Islam.

Part II Oral Practice

Task 1 Group Discussion

Divide the class into small groups and discuss whether there are students in the class who believe in the religion and express their opinions on the role of the religion in the society. Then report his/her opinions to the class.

Task 2 Role Play

Work in groups of 4 or 5. One of you is a tour guide. The rest are visitors. Suppose the tour guide is leading these visitors in different religious places, such as Thailand (Buddhism), Mt. Wudang (Taoism) and the Persian Gulf (Islam). The tour gride is supposed to give a detailed introduction to these religions.

Part III Translation

Task 1 Translate the following words or phrases into English.

(1) 宗教信仰
(2) 觉悟
(3) 长生不死
(4) 儒家思想
(5) 炼丹
(6) 先知
(7) 一神论
(8) 禅经
(9) 德
(10) 得道成仙

Task 2 Translate the following paragraph into English.

儒、释、道三教中,儒与道乃本土文化,而佛教则是源于印度。 然而,在华夏民族强大无比的影响下,形成了儒、释、道三教和谐有利的共存(co-existence)局面,从而构成了光辉灿烂的华夏民族文化,为人类社会的文明和思想做出不可替代的(irreplaceable)贡献。

实用导游英语

Task 3 Translate the following paragraph into Chinese.

All religions, major or minor, must adjust to a world very different from the one in which they arose. Secularism and science have great influence, although less in the developing nations than in those that are industrialized. Although science may weaken religion in some ways, it also brings about new possibilities for spreading it.

导游技巧和业务
Professional Tour Guiding Knowledge & Skills

法定标识

中国国旗 (National Flag)

- 五星红旗是《中华人民共和国宪法》规定的中华人民共和国国旗,由曾联松于1949年7月设计。
- 图案:该旗帜为红底长方形,左上方缀有五颗黄色的五角星,其中四颗小星环拱于大星之右,并各有一个角尖正对大星的中心。
- 涵义
  - "红色"旗面:表示热烈,象征革命;
  - "黄色"五星:象征光明,且象征中国人为黄种人;
  - 一颗"大五角星":代表中国共产党;
  - 四颗"小五角星":代表农民、工人、小资产阶级、民族资产阶级四个阶级;
  - "众星拱辰"格局:象征在中国共产党领导下的各族人民大团结和人民对党的衷心拥护。

中国国徽 (National Emblem)

- 中华人民共和国国徽是中国主权的象征和标志。1950年9月20日,毛泽东主席命令公布中华人民共和国国徽。
- 图案内容:中华人民共和国国旗、天安门、齿轮和麦稻穗。
- 涵义
  - 齿轮、麦稻穗象征工人阶级与农民阶级;
  - 天安门象征新的民族精神:既是五四运动的发源地,又是中华人民共和国成立时举行开国大典的盛大场所；
- 国旗上的五星,代表中国共产党领导下的中国人民大团结；
- 整个图案鲜明地表达了,新中国的性质是工人阶级领导的以工农联盟为基础的人民民主专政的社会主义国家。

中国国歌 (National Anthem)

☞ 中华人民共和国国歌为《义勇军进行曲》。
☞ 1949年9月27日,中国人民政治协商会议第一届全体会议通过决议,以田汉作词、聂耳作曲的《义勇军进行曲》为国歌。
☞ 涵义
- 《义勇军进行曲》诞生于民族危亡关头的1935年。自诞生以来,在人民中广为传唱。它不仅是20世纪30年代中国人民英勇奋斗、不怕流血牺牲的形象概括,更是中华民族勇敢、坚毅、团结和充满必胜信心的斗争精神的体现。
- 新中国成立后,把这首歌作为国歌,为发扬抗日战争期间英勇无畏的精神,也体现了中国人民的革命传统和居安思危的思想。

中国旅游徽志 (China's Tourism Emblem)

☞ 中国旅游业的图形标志为1985年确立的"马超龙雀"。
☞ "马超龙雀"是1969年在甘肃武威出土的东汉时期的一件青铜制品。
☞ 含义
- 选择"马超龙雀"作为中国旅游业的图形标志,含义是天马行空、逸兴腾飞,无所羁缚,象征前程似锦的中国旅游业；
- 马是古今旅游的重要工具,是奋进的象征,旅游者可以在中国尽兴旅游；
- "马超龙雀"青铜制品,象征着中国数千年光辉灿烂的文化与历史,显示文明古国的伟大形象,吸引全世界的旅游者。

中国旅游标志

小贴士

天安门广场升旗仪式

◆ 升降国旗有准确的时间,即要与太阳一同升起、一同降落。这一特殊时间所传递的象征意义是"祖国与日月同辉"。

◆ 新的国旗升降仪式由36名武警官兵组成的国旗护卫队来操演。仪式分节日与平时两套方案执行:每逢重大节日和每月的1日为节日升旗,由62人组成的军乐队现场演奏《歌唱祖国》乐曲,升旗时奏《义勇军进行曲》,平时升旗播放国歌录音。

带领游客观看天安门广场升、降旗仪式,注意事项有哪些?

◆ 参观前一天务必查清升、降旗仪式准确时间;
◆ 安排好时间,提前通知司机;
◆ 安排好客人的叫早时间;
◆ 提前交待注意事项;
◆ 必须保证旅游团的安全。

Discussion & Exercise

Task 1   Can you describe Chinese National Flag?

Task 2   What is the emblem of China's tourism? What is its connotation?

Task 3   Complete the following sentences by translating the Chinese in the brackets into English.

1. The big yellow star on Chinese National Flag represents _____ (中国共产党).
2. On our National Day, a special _____ (升旗仪式) will be held on Tian'anmen Square.
3. On special occasions, _____ (军乐队) will perform the national anthem during the flag raising ceremony.
4. Can you sing our Chinese _____ (国歌)?
5. _____ (国徽) strikingly manifests the nature of the People's Republic of China.

6. Do you know the _____ (中国旅游徽志)?
7. The national flag will be raised every morning _____ (日出时).
8. You can have a very clear view of the flag raising ceremony on _____ (天安门城楼).

Case Study

Some overseas tourists always seem to want to discuss controversial (有争议的) topics with their tour guides, such as human rights, religious policy, Taiwan, Tibet or the Diaoyu Islands. The purpose of the tourists' questions and discussions are quite different; some are out of curiosity, while others bear malicious intentions.

Questions
1. How does a guide handle controversial topics like human rights and religious policy in China?
2. How do you deal with sensitive subjects like Tibet, Taiwan and the Diaoyu Islands?

拓展视频

1. 土生土长的道教
2. 佛教圣地五台山
3. 民俗大观——民间俗神信仰

Unit 9   Traditional Chinese Medicine

▶▶ 导读

中国传统医学博大精深，其独特的诊断手法、系统的治疗方式和丰富的典籍材料，备受世界瞩目。中医讲求望、闻、问、切，使用中药、针灸、推拿、按摩、拔罐、气功、食疗等多种治疗手段，使人体达到阴阳调和而康复。

WARM-UP QUESTIONS

Do you know what the following pictures are showing? Can you tell what kind of aspects of China they represent? Talk about them with your partners.

Unit 9 Traditional Chinese Medicine

Text A

Traditional Chinese Medicine

Based on a tradition of more than 2,000 years, traditional Chinese medicine has established a unique system of prevention and treatment of diseases as well as health maintenance. The formation of traditional Chinese medicine dates back to the Warring States Period and the Qin and Han dynasties. During the long course of its development, the ancient medical experts made substantial contributions together with their works. The Four Great Classic of Traditional Chinese Medicine are *Huangdi's Canon of Medicine* (Huangdi Neijing), *Classic of Difficulties* (Nanjing), *Treaties on Cold Damage and Miscellaneous Disease* (Shanghan Zabing Lun) and *Shennong's Classic of Materia Medica* (Shennong Bencao Jing). ①

Based on the traditional Chinese philosophy, traditional Chinese medicine views the human body as an organic whole made up of primary functional entities, such as gas, blood, meridian joints, and believes that health is a state of correct balance between Yin and Yang.②

Different from the western medicine, which is based on the microscopic and pathologic anatomy, traditional Chinese medicine attributes the occurrence of diseases to climatic changes, environmental variations, imbalance of diet and life, etc. Owing to these factors, once the balance between Yin and Yang is disturbed, diseases appear.

To help restore the body's Yin and Yang balance, traditional Chinese medicine diagnoses through inspection, smelling, inquiry and palpation and uses mainly herbal medicine, acupuncture, moxibustion, massage, cupping, qigong, diet and other therapies.③ Inspection means the observation of the body, complexion, tongue and so on. Smelling refers to analysis of the odor brought by certain diseases. Inquiry is to provide the basis for

Vocabulary

meridian 经络
microscopic 显微的
pathologic 病理的
anatomy 解剖
palpation 把脉

dialectical method and palpation is to identify the rise and fall of internal organ function by examining the pulse change.

Traditional Chinese medicine takes the unparalleled dominant position in treating chronic inflammation, chronic pains, functional disorders④, problems of immune system, sub-health state⑤ and other health problems. Great progress has been made in theoretical and clinical research with the advancement of modern science and technology since the founding of the People's Republic of China. As an integral part of the Chinese culture, traditional Chinese medicine also enjoys a high reputation for integrated theoretical system, rich practical experience and good clinical effect in the rest of the world.

chronic 慢性的
inflammation 炎症
immune 免疫

Notes

1. The Four Great Classic of Traditional Chinese Medicine are *Huangdi's Canon* of Medicine (Huangdi Neijing), *Classic of Difficulties* (Nanjing), *Treaties on Cold Damage and Miscellaneous Disease* (Shanghan Zabing Lun) and *Shennong's Classic of Materia Medica* (Shennong Bencao Jing).《黄帝内经》、《难经》、《伤寒杂病论》和《神农本草经》被视作中医的四大经典。

2. Based on the traditional Chinese philosophy, traditional Chinese medicine views the human body as an organic whole made up of primary functional entities, such as gas, blood, meridian joints, and believes that health is a state of correct balance between Yin and Yang. 基于中国哲学,中医认为人体是由基础的功能体,诸如气、血和经络关节构成的有机个体,而健康就是阴阳的平衡状态。

3. Chinese medicine diagnoses through inspection, smelling, inquiry and palpation and uses mainly the herbal medicine, acupuncture, moxibustion, massage, cupping, qigong, diet and other therapies 中医通过望、闻、问、切进行诊断,并主要使用中药、针灸、艾灸、推拿、拔罐、气功、食疗等方法进行治疗

4. functional disorders 功能紊乱

5. sub-health state 亚健康状态

Unit 9 Traditional Chinese Medicine

Text B   *Chinese Acupuncture*

Acupuncture is a healing technique used in traditional Chinese medicine.① The first known acupuncture text is *Nei Ching Su Wen*. The book is also known by a variety of alternative titles such as the *Yellow Emperor's Classic of Internal Medicine*, or the *Canon of Medicine*;② however, all these titles refer to the same basic text. Acupuncture has a clearly recorded history of about 2,000 years, but some authorities claim that it has been practiced in China for some 4,000 years.

According to traditional Chinese medicine, the human body can be viewed as a system of energy flows.③ When these flows are balanced, the body is healthy. So practitioners of Chinese medicine will take their patients' pulses and examine their tongues to diagnose and talk about energy imbalances.④ Their language may sound very strange, such as "yin deficiency" or "liver heat rising".⑤ The Chinese words Yin and Yang refer to opposing energies that should be in balance, and Qi can be roughly translated as "energy" or "life force". In traditional Chinese medicine, there are many ways to improve the balance of body's energy flows, one of which is acupuncture.

Vocabulary

acupuncture 针灸
alternative 选择性的
canon 经书
flow 流动，通
pulse 脉搏
diagnose 诊断
imbalance 不平衡
deficiency 缺乏，不足
acupuncturist 针灸医生
pathway 通道
meridian 经络
tingle 麻刺感
numbness 麻木，麻痹
nausea 反胃，呕吐，晕船

According to the patients' energy imbalances, the acupuncturist uses very thin needles to stimulate specific points in the body.⑥ These points lie on energy pathways which are called "meridians". ⑦ Acupuncture treatments are designed to improve the flow and balance of energy along these meridians. The patient lies on a table, either on his stomach or on his back. When the needles are inserted at the selected points, the patient may feel a little pain, then tingling or numbness as the needles are inserted. The needles are left in place for up to 30 or 45 minutes, depending on what the acupuncture is intended to accomplish.

Since the research on acupuncture shows that it is effective in treating some kinds of pain and nausea, the National Institutes of Health, in 1997, issued a statement supporting the value of acupuncture for certain conditions. Additionally, the World Health Organization also lists over 40 conditions that may be helped by acupuncture.⑧

The origin of Chinese medicine is a fascinating story and acupuncture represents only one facet of the medical system. With more and more people began to realize the magic power of Chinese traditional medicine, acupuncture will be brought into a new stage in the world of health care.

fascinating 迷人的
represent 象征,代表

Notes

1. Acupuncture is a healing technique used in traditional Chinese medicine. 针灸是中国传统医学中所采用的一种治疗方法。

2. The book is also known by a variety of alternative titles such as the *Yellow Emperor's Classic of Internal Medicine*, or the *Canon of Medicine*... 这本书还有其他许多的名字,譬如《黄帝内经》,或是《药经》……

3. According to traditional Chinese medicine, the human body can be viewed as a system of energy flows. 根据中国传统医学,人体被看做是一种经络体系。

4. So practitioners of Chinese medicine will take their patients' pulses and examine their tongues to diagnose and talk about energy imbalances. 所以中医便会把脉、观舌,从而诊断出病人的能量失衡。

5. Their language may sound very strange, such as "yin deficiency" or "liver heat rising". 中医所使用的语言会有些怪异,例如"阴气不足","肝火上升"。

6. According to the patients' energy imbalances, the acupuncturist uses very thin needles to stimulate specific points in the body. 根据病人的能量失衡,针灸师使用非常细的针来扎刺人体的某些穴位。

7. These points lie on the energy pathways which are called "meridians". 在人体能量通道上的这些点被称为"经络"。

8. Additionally, the World Health Organization also lists over 40 conditions that may be helped by acupuncture. 此外,世界卫生组织也列出四十多种可以使用针灸治疗的疾病。

Unit 9 Traditional Chinese Medicine

Text C

Chinese Herbal Medicine

Vocabulary

component 成分
fundamental 基础的，基本的
diagnosis 诊断
symptom 症状
nourish 滋养，使健壮
ailment 疾病
prescribe 处方，开药
powder 粉末
tincture 酊剂
contaminant 玷污物，污染物
compile 汇编
pharmacopoeia 药典

Chinese herbal medicine is a major component of traditional Chinese medicine and is based on the concepts of Yin and Yang along with other branches of Chinese medicine, such as acupuncture. It aims to understand in which way the fundamental balance and harmony between the two (Yin and Yang) may be undermined, and then focuses on restoring a balance of energy, body and spirit to maintain health, rather than treating a particular disease or medical condition.① Clinical strategies are based upon diagnosis of patterns of signs and symptoms that reflect an imbalance and herbs are used with the goal of restoring balance by nourishing the body.

Chinese herbal medicine uses a variety of herbs to restore balance of energy to the body. Some herbs such as Ginkgo, Ginseng, Green Tea and Siberian Ginseng are said to prevent and treat hormone disturbances, infections, breathing disorders, and a vast number of other ailments and diseases.② There are even some practitioners who claim that the herbs have the power to prevent and treat a variety of cancers.

Herbs are now available in a number of formats, both traditional and modern. The traditional method is to boil a mixture of dried herbs to make a tea or to make pills. The herbs are also now commonly prescribed as freeze dried powders or tinctures.③ For those who have never tried them before, the herbs taste at first unusual and often bitter, but the vast majority of people will get used to the taste very quickly.

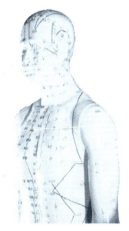

Generally speaking, Chinese herbs are very safe when prescribed correctly by a properly trained practitioner. Practitioners of traditional Chinese medicine are licensed by a state board that can provide advice on sources of herbs less likely to contain dangerous contaminants. Over centuries, doctors have compiled detailed information about the pharma-copoeia and placed great emphasis on the protection of patients.④

However, although the long history of traditional Chinese herbal

实用导游英语

dose 剂量
supervision 监督,管理
guidance 指导
capacity 能力
well-being 健康

medicine sometimes can be treated as evidence of safety, it is important to note that many of these herbs are no longer produced and used as they were in the past. The reason for this is that using low doses of an herb for a short period of time under close supervision of a traditional practitioner in the past does not ensure that these herbs are safe to use; this is particularly true when they are taken in high doses and concentrated forms over a longer period of time without medical guidance.⑤

By and large, Chinese traditional medicine as a whole places great emphasis on lifestyle management in order to prevent disease before it occurs. Chinese medicine recognizes that health is more than just the absence of disease.⑥ It is believed that Chinese herb has a unique capacity to maintain and enhance our capacity for well-being and happiness.

Notes

1. It aims to understand in which way the fundamental balance and harmony between the two (Yin and Yang) may be undermined, and then focuses on restoring a balance of energy, body and spirit to maintain health, rather than treating a particular disease or medical condition. 中国中草药学旨在理解阴阳的基本平衡与和谐会遭到何种方式的破坏,然后专注于恢复能量、体力和精神的平衡从而保持健康,而不是对某种疾病或是健康状况的治疗。

2. Some herbs such as Ginkgo, Ginseng, Green Tea and Siberian Ginseng are said to prevent and treat hormone disturbances, infections, breathing disorders and a vast number of other ailments and diseases. 一些中药,诸如银杏、人参、绿茶和西洋参等据称可以预防和治疗多种疾病,如荷尔蒙失调、感染、呼吸性疾病及其他各种各样的疾病。

3. The herbs are also now commonly prescribed as freeze dried powders or tinctures. 中药的处方也常常为冻干剂或者酊剂。

4. Over centuries, doctors have compiled detailed information about the pharmacopoeia and placed great emphasis on the protection of the patients. 数百年来,医生们编撰了许多内容详细的药典,并且非常重视对病人的保护。

5. The reason for this is that using low doses of an herb for a short period of time under close supervision of a traditional practitioner in the past does not ensure that these herbs are safe to use; this is particularly true when they are taken in high doses and concentrated forms over a longer period of time without medical guidance. 原因在于,过去是在传统中医大夫的指导下短时间小剂量的服用中药,而现在变为长时间大剂量的集中服用中药,无法保证用药安全。

Unit 9 Traditional Chinese Medicine

6. Chinese medicine recognizes that health is more than just the absence of disease. 中医认为健康不仅仅是没有疾病。

Useful Phrases and Expressions

1. alternative titles 其他的名称
2. take somebody's pulse 把脉
3. bring something to a new stage 将某物带入一个崭新的阶段
4. prevention and treatment of diseases 疾病防治
5. health maintenance 保健
6. imbalance of diet 饮食不均衡
7. immune system 免疫系统
8. keep/ break the balance of energy of body 保持/打破身体能量的均衡
9. hormone disturbance 荷尔蒙失调
10. breathing disorder 呼吸紊乱

Exercises

Part I Listening Practice

Passage 1

Shaolin Temple and Shaolin Kungfu

unavoidably 不可避免地
descendant 后代，继承者
imitate 模仿
Kungfu 功夫
mediation 冥想

Task 1 Listen to the passage carefully and then fill in the blanks with what you hear. The passage will be read only once.

Bruce Lee, Jet Li or Jackie Chan, all famous Chinese film stars adept in Wushu are great names in the world. Anyone who has seen _____1_____ Chinese Kungfu movies will be deeply impressed by the Chinese Wushu, which is called Kungfu or Chinese _____2_____ arts in the West.

People, home or abroad, are unavoidably amazed by Chinese Kungfu _____3_____ in "Crouching Tiger, Hidden Dragon". Anyone interested in Kungfu has heard of Shaolin Temple (Shaolin Si), which is _____4_____ as the birth place of Kungfu.

Shaolin Kungfu is the very first martial arts ever created. If you try to _____5_____ the roots of all martial arts in existence, you will eventually reach Shaolin, as all martial arts are either a direct or _____6_____ descendant of Shaolin Kungfu. Shaolin monks have been practicing Kungfu for over 1500 years.

Shaolin Temple is located at the south foot of Songshan Mountain. It is said that Da Mo, seeing monks becoming fat from long hours sitting in meditation, came up with the idea of walking _____7_____, which imitated the natural motions of _____8_____ and birds. Eventually, the imitation evolved into a form of unarmed _____9_____ or martial arts, which is known as Kungfu. Da Mo taught the monks of Shaolin basic routines to improve their health and to _____10_____ themselves.

Task 2 Listen to the recording again and then answer the following questions.

(1) Who are Bruce Lee, Jet Li and Jackie Chan?

(2) Why Shaolin Kungfu is famous to anyone who are interested in Chinese martial arts?

(3) Where is Shaolin Temple?

(4) Who created Shaolin Kungfu?

(5) How was Shaolin Kungfu created?

Unit 9 Traditional Chinese Medicine

Passage 2

Chinese Herbs in Modern Society

enslave 奴役
susceptible 敏感的
tribal 部落的
pharmacy 药店
rhythmic 有节奏的
invasion 侵略,侵占
formulation 药方

Task 1 Listen to the passage carefully and then fill in the blanks with what you hear. The passage will be read only once.

Most people today live under great _____1_____ from their families, jobs and themselves. Though it is commonly accepted that a good health calls for a healthier _____2_____, it is rather difficult to achieve in reality.

The following words come from the *Neijing*, a Chinese _____3_____ classic which was written some 2,000 years ago, but they could _____4_____ well apply today, "People are enslaved by their _____5_____ and worries. They work too hard in heavy labor. They do not follow the rhythmic changes of the four seasons and thus become susceptible to the invasion of the winds."

However, the traditional Chinese herbs can help the heavy-pressured people to _____6_____ their health and their balance of energy. Native cultures all over the world have traditionally used herbs to _____7_____ health and treat illnesses. Chinese herbal medicine developed with Chinese culture from tribal roots. By 200 BC, traditional Chinese medicine was firmly _____8_____, and by the first century AD, a listing of medicinal herbs and herbal formulations had been developed.

With the increase in _____9_____ of herbal use, many Chinese herbs are sold individually and in formulas. In the United States, Chinese herbs and herbal formulas may be purchased in health food stores, some pharmacies and from _____10_____ medicine practitioners.

Task 2 Have you got a clear idea of Chinese Herbs? Tell each other the importance of Chinese herbs in modern society without looking at the textbook.

Part II Oral Practice

Task 1 Group Discussion

Divide the class into small groups and each student will give his/her opinions on the traditional Chinese medicine. Do they think that the traditional Chinese medicine will have a bright future or will be replaced even disappear with modernization? Exchange ideas with their partners, and then report his/her opinions to the class.

Task 2 Role Play

Work in groups of 4 or 5. One of you is a tour guide. The rest are foreign visitors who are very interested in Chinese Wushu and Chinese herbs. The tour guide is going to introduce these parts of traditional Chinese cultural heritage to them to help them have a better understanding of China's long and glorious history.

Part III Translation

Task 1 Translate the following words or phrases into English.

(1) 黄帝内经   (2) 把脉
(3) 人体经络   (4) 阴阳平衡
(5) 慢性疾病   (6) 气候变化
(7) 望、闻、问、切   (8) 气色
(9) 中草药   (10) 健康幸福

Task 2 Translate the following paragraph into English.

华佗被认为是一位神医,受人崇拜。"华佗在世"是对一个高度熟练的医生的尊重。华佗创造的疗法和健身方法,是中国医学史上的一个里程碑,具有十分重要的意义。华佗被后人尊称为"外科鼻祖"。

Unit 9 Traditional Chinese Medicine

Task 3　Translate the following paragraph into Chinese.

The first recorded attempt at conceptualizing（定义）and treating disease dates back to about 1500 BC During the Shang Dynasty. The philosophical basis of much of the very early Chinese medicine seems to have tried to seek a harmony between the living and their dead ancestors, and the good and evil spirits that inhabited（居住在）the earth.

Professional Tour Guiding Knowledge & Skills

航空知识

机票常识

☞ 客票
- 旅客购票,需提供本人有效身份证件;
- 只限票上所列姓名的旅客本人使用,不得转让和涂改,否则客票无效,票款不退;
- 正常票价的客票有效期为一年。

☞ 儿童票
- 12周岁以下的儿童,按成人全票价的50%购票;
- 未满两周岁的婴儿,按成人全票价的10%购票,不单独占座位;每一成人旅客只能有一个婴儿享受这种票价,超过的人数应购买儿童票。

☞ 机舱等级
- 头等舱 (F, first class)
- 公务舱 (C, business class)
- 经济舱 (Y, economy class)

☞ 座位确认 (air ticket confirmation)
- OPEN票:指不确定日期的回程机票,即指定航班,但航班日期不定。持OPEN票是不能随时登机的,需在航班起飞前72小时,向航空公司对订座进行确认。经过座位确认,就成了OK票;
- OK票:指已确定好日期、航班和机座的飞机票。OK票也可以改日期,但要收取手续费。

实用导游英语

☞ 退票
- 旅客要求退票,按不同时段,缴纳不等的退票费。

乘机须知
☞ 办理手续
- 旅客应在航空公司规定的时限内到达机场,凭客票和有效身份证件,办理乘机手续。航班离站前30分钟,停止办理乘机手续。

☞ 安全检查 (security check)
- 旅客所携带的行李物品,在登机前必须接受安全检查。

☞ 误机
- 旅客误机,需在原航班起飞时间的次日中午12时前,进行误机确认。误机旅客可以要求改乘后续航班;若要求退票,须支付相当于票价50%的误机费。

☞ 航班不正常服务
- 因航空公司的原因,造成航班延误或取消,航空公司免费向旅客提供食宿等服务;
- 由于天气等不可抗拒的因素,在始发站造成延误或取消,航空公司可协助旅客安排食宿,费用由旅客自理。

行李托运 (luggage check-in)
☞ 随身携带物品
- 旅客随身携带物品的体积不超过20×40×55厘米,重量不超过5千克。

☞ 免费行李额
- 持成人或儿童票的旅客,每人可免费托运行李:头等舱40千克,公务舱30千克,经济舱20千克;
- 持婴儿票的旅客,无免费行李额。

☞ 相关规定
- 按照规定,查看是否有不准作为行李运输的物品,不准在托运行李中夹带的物品等,并遵照规定办理。

禁止携带下列物品
THE FOLLOWING OBJECTS IS NOT PERMITTED

枪支 FIREARMS　弹药 AMMUNITION　警械 POLICEWEAPONS　管制刀具 CONTROLLED KNIFE　放射物品 RADIOACTIVE
易燃易爆 FLAMMABLE EXPLOSIVES　腐蚀品 CORROSIVES　毒害品 POISONS　氧化剂 OXIDISING　强磁物品 MAGNETIZED

Unit 9 Traditional Chinese Medicine

> **小贴士**
>
> **带领游客乘机时,导游的工作有哪些?**
> - 制订好离店计划,提前通知酒店;
> - 检查、确认机票起飞时间;
> - 提醒行李是否带齐;
> - 带领游客提前到达机场;
> - 收齐机票、护照(身份证)、团体签证、出入境表格等;
> - 为全团办理登机手续;
> - 托运全团行李并保管好行李票;
> - 分发登机牌并归还证件;
> - 带领游客通关(安检);
> - 带领游客登机。

Discussion & Exercise

Task 1 What kind of articles cannot be taken on the plane?

Task 2 How much check-in luggage is allowed for an international flight?

Task 3 Complete the following sentences by translating the Chinese in the brackets into English.

1. The tour escort must gather the plane tickets, passports, the group visa and the _____ _____ (出入境表格).
2. In most cases, _____ (包机飞行) are cheaper than regular airlines.
3. It was announced that the flight from London had been delayed due to _____ (恶劣天气).
4. Passengers cannot get _____ (赔偿) for the delay due to natural disasters.
5. Attention please! Flight MU5401 to Bangkok _____ (正在登机).
6. The plane was cancelled due to _____ (不可抗力因素), and we got nothing in compensation.
7. The passengers must take care of their _____ (手提行李).
8. Every passenger must go through the _____ (安检).

# Case Study

Sophie took a European group to the airport for their flight to Paris. One tourist had an open ticket. He could not board the plane as it was full. He had to take the next day's flight.

Questions
1. What's an open ticket?
2. What should tourists be notified of so as to avoid the above situation?

1. 民族瑰宝：中医
2. 百年老店：同仁堂
3. 民俗大观——养生文化

Unit 10　Folklore

▶▶ 导读

> 中国古典文学宝库中,除了有史书记载的古典文学作品外,还有一类是民间神话传说,数量众多,内容丰富,绚丽多彩,充满诗情画意和艺术魅力。其中《牛郎织女》、《孟姜女》、《嫦娥奔月》、《梁山伯与祝英台》、《女娲补天》、《大禹治水》、《白蛇传》、《愚公移山》等都广为流传,它们和其他民间传说故事构成了中国民间文化的一个重要组成部分。

WARM-UP QUESTIONS

Do you know what story each of the following pictures tells? Which Chinese folk story do you like best? Do you know some other folk stories besides these? Talk about them with your partners.

Text A

Cowherd and Weaving Girl

Vocabulary

diligent 勤奋的
orphan 孤儿
buffalo 水牛
relieve 减轻
Cowherd 牛郎
celestial 天庭的，天上的
restrictive 限制的
earthly 俗世的
sneak 偷跑
weave 编织
trace 追赶，追踪
wrath 愤怒
hide (动物的)皮

Long long ago, there was a young man who was very clever, diligent and honest. But at an early age, he became an orphan and lived a very poor life. However, one day, he adopted an abandoned old buffalo, and everything changed.① The buffalo was very loyal and relieved the young man from much of the hard labor in the fields. They enjoyed a very good relationship with each other, being seen together all the time.② So, the villagers from far and near came to know him by the name of the Cowherd③.

Meanwhile, in heaven, the youngest of the seven celestial princesses had grown tired of the privileged but restrictive life in the heavenly palace. She longed for an earthly life. So, one day, she determined to pursue her own happiness. She sneaked out and descended onto the earth④. She met the Cowherd with whom she had secretly fallen in love all along in heaven.

They married and had a lovely boy and a lovely girl. While the Cowherd worked in the fields with his old pal—the buffalo—the heavenly princess weaved at home to support the family. Villagers all admired her excellent weaving skill and started learning from her. She was now well-known as the Weaving Girl.

The family lived happily until the girl's celestial royal family found her missing and traced her to the village. The Celestial Empress was in such a wrath that she gave her daughter only two choices: to go back to heaven or to see her husband and children destroyed. The weaving girl had no choice but to leave.

Just at that time, the old buffalo suddenly began to speak to the astonished Cowherd, saying that it was dying in no time and asking the man to use its hide as a vehicle to fly into the

134

heaven to get his wife ⑤. Then the Cowherd sailed off to heaven with his young son and daughter in two baskets.

Fearing that the young man would catch up, the Empress took out her hair spin and drew a big river (Silvery River) across the sky, intending to separate the family forever.⑥ However, all the magpies in the world, deeply touched by the story, came to their rescue. Each year, on the seventh day of the seventh month, they would flock together to form a bridge so that the family may enjoy a brief reunion.⑦

hair spin 发簪
Silver River 银河
magpie 鹊，喜鹊
rescue 拯救

Notes

1. However, one day, he adopted an abandoned old buffalo, and everything changed. 但是，有一天，他收留了一只被人遗弃的老牛，从此一切改变了。
2. They enjoyed a very good relationship with each other, being seen together all the time. 他们之间其乐融融，人们总是能看见他俩待在一起。
3. the villagers from far and near came to know him by the name of the Cowherd 所以远近村子里的村民都开始叫他牛郎
4. determined to pursue her own happiness, she sneaked out and descended onto the earth（织女）下定决心追求自己的幸福，所以她悄悄地离开天庭，下凡到人间
5. saying that it was dying in no time and asking the man to use its hide as a vehicle to fly into the heaven to get his wife（老牛）说它马上就要死了，它让牛郎在它死后，披上它的牛皮，便能飞上天去追赶他的妻子
6. Fearing that the young man would catch up, the Empress took out her hair spin and drew a big river (Silvery River) across the sky, intending to separate the family forever. 王母害怕牛郎会追上来，所以她便摘下她的发簪，然后在天空中划出一条河（银河），企图永远地将这一家人分开。
7. Each year, on the seventh day of the seventh month, they would flock together to form a bridge so that the family may enjoy a brief reunion. 每年，在（阴历）七月初七，喜鹊便会飞到一起，搭座鹊桥，让这一家人能够有个短暂的重聚。

Text B

Meng Jiangnv

Vocabulary

yard 院子

This story happened during the Qin Dynasty (221BC—207BC). Meng Jiangnv was a beautiful, kind-hearted young woman. One day while playing in the yard, Meng Jiangnv saw a young man hiding in the garden.

实用导游英语

good-mannered 行为举止良好的
wed 嫁,结婚
sew 缝纫
farewell 再见
pack 打包
whereabouts 地点,下落
exhaustion 劳累
collapse 倒塌
wail 哭泣
enrage 愤怒
suppress 压制,压抑
terms 条款,条件
funeral 葬礼
black mourning 黑色葬服
reluctantly 犹豫的

She called out to her parents, and the young man whose name was Fan Qiliang came out.

Fan Qiliang was an intellectual man. At that time, Emperor Qin Shi Huang announced that he intended to build the Great Wall.① So lots of men were caught by the Emperor's officials. Fan was very afraid of being caught, so he went to Meng's house to hide from the officials. Meng Jiangnv's parents liked this good-looking, honest and good-mannered young man so much that they decided to wed their daughter to him.② Both Fan Qiliang and Meng Jiangnv accepted happily, and the couple was married several days later. However, three days after their marriage, officials suddenly broke in and took Fan Qiliang away to build the Great Wall in the north of China.

It was a hard time for Meng Jiangnv after her husband was taken away.③ She missed her husband and cried nearly every day. She sewed warm clothes for her husband and decided to set off to look for him. Saying farewell to her parents, she packed her luggage and started her long journey. After days and nights of hardship, she finally reached the foot of the Great Wall at the present Shanhaiguan Pass.

Upon her arrival, she was anxious to ask about her husband's whereabouts.④ Bad news came to her, however, that Fan Qiliang had already died of exhaustion and was buried into the Great Wall! Meng Jiangnv could not help crying. She sat on the ground and cried and cried. Suddenly with a tremendous noise, a 400-kilometer-long section of the Great Wall collapsed over her bitter wail.⑤ Emperor Qin Shi Huang was enraged and ready to punish the woman.

However, at the first sight of Meng Jiangnv, Emperor Qin Shi Huang was attracted by her beauty. Instead of killing her, the Emperor asked Meng Jiangnv to marry him. Suppressing her feeling of anger, Meng Jiangnv agreed on the basis of three terms.⑥ The first was to find the body of Fan Qiliang; the second was to hold a state funeral for him; and the last one was to have Emperor Qin Shi Huang wear black mourning for Fan Qiliang and attend the funeral in person⑦. Emperor Qin Shi Huang thought for a while and reluctantly agreed. After all the terms were met, Emperor Qin Shi Huang was ready to

136

Unit 10 Folklore

take her to his palace.⑧ When the guards were not watching, she suddenly turned around and jumped into the nearby Bohai Sea.

Notes

1. At that time, Emperor Qin Shi Huang announced that he intended to build the Great Wall. 当时,秦始皇下令修建长城。

2. Meng Jiangnv's parents liked this good-looking, honest and good-mannered young man so much that they decided to wed their daughter to him. 孟姜女的父母非常喜欢这个长相俊俏,诚实有礼貌的年轻人,所以他们决定把自己的女儿许配给他。

3. It was a hard time for Meng Jiangnv after her husband was taken away. 孟姜女在丈夫被官差带走后,整日悲伤难过。

4. Upon her arrival, she was anxious to ask about her husband's whereabouts. 孟姜女一到地方,便四处打听丈夫的下落。

5. Suddenly with a tremendous noise, a 400-kilometer-long section of the Great Wall collapsed over her bitter wail. 突然天地之间一声巨响,绵延400千米的一段长城在孟姜女的悲泣中顷刻坍塌化为灰烬。

6. Suppressing her feeling of anger, Meng Jiangnv agreed on the basis of three terms. 孟姜女强压怒火,答应只要秦始皇能够满足她的三个条件(她便嫁给他)。

7. the second was to hold a state funeral for him; and the last one was to have Emperor Qin Shi Huang wear black mourning for Fan Qiliang and attend the funeral in person 第二个条件是秦始皇必须为自己的丈夫举行国葬,最后一个条件便是秦始皇需亲自身穿葬服出席葬礼

8. After all the terms were met, Emperor Qin Shi Huang was ready to take her to his palace. 等到三个条件都做到后,秦始皇准备带孟姜女回宫。

Text C

Legend of Chang E

The Jade Emperor in Heaven wished to help farmers raise animals and cultivate their fields, so he gave orders to his ten sons to become ten suns and travel across the sky one at a time, each taking one day.① But the ten young men disobeyed; all ten of them came out every day, and the heat from ten suns shining all at once made the earth intolerably hot.

The Jade Emperor saw the destruction caused by his sons. He sent Hou Yi, his bravest god, down to earth to solve the problem of the ten

Vocabulary
disobey 不服从
intolerably 难以忍受地
destruction 破坏
catastrophe 灾难

| bow 弓
| obedience 服从
| furious 愤怒的
| mortal 凡人
| wrinkle 皱纹
| goddess 女神
| instruct 教导,指导
| attain 达到,得到
| abandon 抛弃
| swallow 吞咽
| image 样子,形象
| maiden 少女

suns and end the catastrophe.② Hou Yi was a good, courageous god with a beautiful wife, Chang E. Chang E didn't like the thought of going down to earth, but she was unwilling to be separated from her husband, so together they descended to earth.

Hou Yi was a great archer and brought his magic bow from Heaven with him. At first, Hou Yi tried to negotiate with the ten suns, but they refused to listen. This angered Hou Yi. He took out his magic bow and arrows and shot down nine of the suns; the last sun begged for his life and promised obedience at performing his task of separating night from day.③ Finally the earth was at peace and people enjoyed their work and lives. However, when Hou Yi made his report to the Jade Emperor, he was furious at Hou Yi for killing his nine sons, and refused to let the Divine Couple return to Heaven④.

Chang E was unhappy to be an earthly mortal with all of mortality's suffering, aging and death in particular.⑤ She was terrified to see wrinkles appearing around her eyes, and demanded that Hou Yi find some way to restore her immortality.

Hou Yi decided to climb Kunlun Mountain and beg the Royal Goddess for the pill of immortality. The Goddess gave him her one remaining pill. She instructed Hou Yi that if one person took the pill he would ascend to Heaven, but if he cut the pill into two halves and shared it with another person they could live forever⑥. The pill had to be taken on the 15th night of the eighth month when the moon was fullest. Hou Yi was very happy and thanked the Royal Goddess and went home to Chang E. They decided to divide the pill and take it at the proper time so that they could both attain immortality.

But on the 15th of the eighth month, Chang Er saw no sign of Hou Yi. She waited and later grew impatient. As the moon rose, thinking that Hou Yi had abandoned her, Chang E swallowed the whole pill. At once she felt her body becoming lighter, rising upwards towards the sky.⑦

Each year on the 15th day of the eighth month, when the moon is at its fullest and brightest, people look at the moon and try to see the image of a beautiful maiden in it.

Unit 10 Folklore

Notes

1. The Jade Emperor in Heaven wished to help the farmers raise animals and cultivate their fields, so he gave orders to his ten sons to become ten suns and travel across the sky one at a time, each taking one day. 天上的玉皇大帝想帮助农夫养畜耕田,于是就派他的十个儿子化为十个太阳,每人一天轮流上天。

2. He sent Hou Yi, his bravest god, down to earth to solve the problem of the ten suns and end the catastrophe. 他派遣最为勇敢的天神后羿来到人间,去解决十个太阳的问题,结束这场灾难。

3. He took out his magic bow and arrows and shot down nine of the suns; the last sun begged for his life and promised obedience at performing his task of separating night from day. 他拿出神弓神箭将九个太阳射落,最后一个太阳求他饶命,并承诺白天值班,使日夜更替。

4. he was furious at Hou Yi for killing his nine sons, and refused to let the Divine Couple return to Heaven 因为后羿杀了他的九个儿子,他大为震怒,拒绝这对神仙美眷重返天宫

5. Chang E was unhappy to be an earthly mortal with all of mortality's suffering, aging and death in particular. 嫦娥不愿意成为凡人,忍受凡人的痛苦,尤其是衰老与死亡。

6. if one person took the pill he would ascend to Heaven, but if he cut the pill into two halves and shared it with another person, they could live forever 若人吃了这药就会升天,但是如果把药分成两半与别人分享的话,这二人就能长生不老

7. As the moon rose, thinking that Hou Yi had abandoned her, Chang E swallowed the whole pill and at once she felt her body becoming lighter, rising upwards towards the sky. 月亮升起,嫦娥认为后羿背叛了自己,于是吞下了整粒药。很快她感到身子变轻,向天上飞去。

Useful Phrases and Expressions

1. know somebody by the name of 叫某人……名字
2. long for 期待,渴望
3. sneak out of 偷偷溜出
4. in a wrath 勃然大怒
5. sail off 起航,出发
6. break in 破门而入
7. take somebody away 带走,抓走某人
8. set off to do something 出发或是着手做某事
9. meet one's terms 满足某人的条件或要求
10. cultivate the fields 耕田
11. end the catastrophe 结束灾难
12. at the proper time 在合适的时机
13. rise upward towards the sky 飞上天

Exercises

Part I Listening Practice

Passage 1

Nv Wa Mends the Sky

Nv Wa 女娲
rage 愤怒，咆哮
devour 吞咽
prey on 以……为食
pacify 使平静
sting 刺

mend 补
fierce 凶残的
vicious 邪恶的
crack 缝隙
poisonous 有毒的

Task 1 Listen to the passage carefully and then fill in the blanks with what you hear. The passage will be read only once.

In ancient times, the four corners of the sky ____1____ and the world with its nine regions ____2____ open. The sky could not cover all the things under it, nor could the earth carry all the things on it. A great fire raged and would not ____3____; a fierce flood raced about and could not be checked. Savage beasts devoured innocent people; vicious birds preyed on ____4____.

Then Nv Wa melted rocks of five ____5____ and used them to mend the cracks in the sky. She supported the four corners of the sky with the legs she had cut off from a giant ____6____. She killed the black dragon to save the people of Jizhou, and blocked the flood with the ____7____ of reeds. Thus the sky was mended, its four corners lifted, the flood ____8____, Jizhou pacified, and harmful birds and beasts killed, and the innocent people were able to live on the square earth under the ____9____ of the sky. It was a time when birds, beasts, insects and snakes no longer used their claws or teeth or poisonous stings, for they did not want to catch or eat weaker things.

Nv Wa's deeds ____10____ the heavens above and the earth below. Her name was remembered by later generations and her light shone on every creation.

Task 2   Listen to the recording again and then answer the following questions.

(1) What happened in the ancient time?

_____

(2) How did Nv Wa mend the cracks in the sky?

_____

(3) What did Nv Wa do to save the people in Jizhou?

_____

(4) Why didn't the birds, beasts, insects and snakes use their claws or teeth or poisonous stings any more?

_____

(5) Why will Nv Wa's name be remembered by all later generations?

_____

Passage 2

Greek Myth and Heroes

Greek myth 希腊神话
heroic 英雄的
supplanting 篡位的
differentiated 不同的

sophistication 成熟，高度发展
obstacle 障碍，阻碍
deity 神，神明

实用导游英语

Task 1 Listen to the passage carefully and then fill in the blanks with what you hear. The passage will be read only once.

It is a ____1____ accepted fact that ancient Greek civilization provided the ____2____ of Western culture. The Greeks reached an astonishing level of sophistication in philosophy, art, science and politics. The deepest ____3____ of Greek ideology, however, lay in a mythology so rich that its legacy has endured to the present day. More often than not, the ____4____ of Greek myths is heroic.

The role of the hero is mapped out in such recurring themes as the ____5____ from the mother, the overcoming of ____6____, and the finding and supplanting of the father. The great heroes whose lives ____7____ this pattern include Perseus, Theseus and Oedipus.

In addition, the Olympian pantheon of gods was the most well-known, each deity possessing a ____8____ character. Twelve of them famously lived on Mount Olympus.

The gods were differentiated from the ____9____ not so much by their strength as by their supernatural power. They demanded worship from heroes and men alike and, in return, were able to perform miracles, offer ____10____ protection, or give magical gifts.

Task 2 Have you got a clear idea of the main theme of Greek myth? Tell each other about the heroes in both Greek myth and Chinese folklore without looking at the textbook.

Part II Oral Practice

Task 1 Group Discussion

Divide the class into small groups and each student will give his/her group members a summary of the folklore mentioned in the texts. Then ask the other students to make some additions if necessary.

Unit 10 Folklore

Task 2 Role Play

Work in groups of 4 or 5. One of you is a tour guide. The rest are foreign visitors. The foreign visitors are very interested in the folklore of each scenic spot. They ask the guide to give them a detailed description of some very well-known Chinese folklore.

Part III Translation

Task 1 Translate the following words or phrases into English.

(1) 牛郎织女   (2) 仙女
(3) 银河   (4) 鹊桥
(5) 国葬   (6) 人间生活
(7) 神仙美眷   (8) 凡人
(9) 玉帝   (10) 升天

Task 2 Translate the following paragraph into English.

《西游记》(*Journey to the West*)是中国四大名著之一，也是男女老少都非常喜欢的民间传说。它讲述的是唐僧师徒(disciples)四人踏上征程，克服种种困难，最后取得真经的故事。其中孙悟空的机智勇敢，猪八戒的好吃懒做以及沙和尚的任劳任怨(hard-working and responsible)都给读者留下了深刻的印象。

Task 3 Translate the following paragraph into Chinese.

In the Age of Gold, the world was first furnished with inhabitants. This was an age of innocence (天真无邪) and happiness. Truth and right prevailed (主宰), though not enforced by law, nor was there any in authority to threaten or to punish bad people. The earth brought forth all things necessary for man, without his labor in plowing (犁地) or sowing (播种).

实用导游英语

导游技巧和业务
Professional Tour Guiding Knowledge & Skills

出入境知识

外国人、华侨、港澳台同胞及中国公民出入我国边境,须持有效出入境证件,至指定口岸接受我国边防检查站(由公安、海关、卫生检疫三方组成)的查验。

有效证件

☞ 护照
- 概念:护照是一国主管机关发给本国公民出国或在国外居留的证件,证明其国籍和身份。
- 分类:外交护照、公务护照和普通护照三种。有的国家为团体出国人员(旅游团、体育队、文艺团队)发放团体护照。
    ◇ 外交护照:发给政府高级官员、国会议员、外交和领事官员,负有特殊外交使命的人员、政府代表团成员等;持有外交护照者在外国享受外交礼遇(如豁免权)。
    ◇ 公务护照:发给政府一般官员,驻外使、领馆工作人员以及因公派往国外执行文化、经济等任务的人员。
    ◇ 普通护照:发给一般公民和国外侨民。又分为因公普通护照和因私普通护照。

- 颁发机构:在中国,外交护照、公务护照由外事部门颁发,普通护照由公安部门颁发。
- 电子护照
    ◇ 自2012年5月15日起,公安机关统一签发电子普通护照;
    ◇ 电子护照和原护照的差别:在旧版普通护照中嵌入电子芯片,芯片中存储有持照人的个人基本资料、相貌、指纹等生物特征;
    ◇ 若旧版普通护照在有效期内,仍可正常使用,无需换发电子普通护照。
- 有效期
    ◇ 护照有一定的有效期限,各个国家所规定的有效期限不同;
    ◇ 2007年1月1日施行的《护照法》规定,我国公民护照有限期以16周岁为界:16周岁以下公民的护照有效期为5年,16周岁以上公民的护照有效期为10年,取消延期。

- ☞ 签证
    - 概念:签证是一国主管机关在本国或外国公民所持的护照或其他旅行证件上签注、盖印,表示准其出入本国国境或者过境的手续;
    - 分类
        - ◎ 世界上大多数国家的签证分为外交签证、公务签证和普通签证种。我国签证分为外交签证、礼遇签证、公务签证和普通签证4种;
        - ◎ 按出入境性质,签证又分为出境签证、入境签证、入出境签证、出入境签证、再入境签证和过境签证6种;
        - ◎ 此外,还有移民签证、非移民签证,另纸签证、口岸签证和ADS(Approved Destination Status)签证等。
    - 旅游签证(tourist visa):属于普通签证,在中国为L字签证(发给来中国旅游、探亲或因其他私人事务入境的人员)。
    - 团体签证:9人以上(不含9人)的旅游团可发放团体签证。团体签证一式三份,签发机关留一份,来华旅游团两份:一份用于入境,一份用于出境使用。
    - 有效期:签证的有效期限不等,获签证者必须在有效期内进入中国境内,超过期限签证则不再有效。
    - 免签:中国与许多国家达成互免签证协议,如:阿根廷、埃及、巴西、俄罗斯、马尔代夫、南非等,主要面向外交护照和公务护照。
- ☞ 港澳居民来往内地通行证(Mainland Travel Permit for Hong Kong and Macao Residents)
    - 概念:由中华人民共和国广东省公安厅签发,是具有中华人民共和国国籍的香港特别行政区及澳门特别行政区居民来往中国内地所用的证件;
    - 有效期:年满18周岁持此证有效期为10年,未满18周岁的为3年。
- ☞ 台湾居民来往大陆通行证(Mainland Travel Permit for Taiwan Residents)
    - 概念:是中华人民共和国政府发给台湾居民来往大陆探亲、旅游、投融资、就业、就学等的证件。

海关手续(Customs Formalities)

- ☞ 出入口岸
    - 外国人、华侨和台湾同胞可持有效证件,在指定的对外开放的口岸出入中国或祖国内地;
    - 香港同胞持证经深圳、澳门同胞持证经珠海通行。

实用导游英语

☞ 海关通道

- 红色通道 (Red Channel: Goods to Declare)：又称应税通道或申报通道，游客需填写"旅客行李申报单"向海关申报，经海关查验后放行；
- 绿色通道 (Green Channel: Nothing to Declare)：又称免税通道或无申报通道，持有外交签证或礼遇签证的人员，可选择此通道通关。

> **小贴士**
>
> 我国海关限制进出境的物品有哪些？
>
> ◇ 限制入境物品：无线电收发信机、通信保密机，烟、酒，濒危的和珍贵的动物、植物(均含标本)及其种子和繁殖材料，国家货币，海关限制入境的其他物品；
>
> ◇ 限制出境物品：金银等贵重金属及其制品，国家货币，外币及其有价证券，无线电收发信机、通信保密机，贵重中药材，一般文物，海关限制出境的其他物品。

Discussion & Exercise

Task 1   How many different types of visa are issued in China?

Task 2   What should a citizen of Hong Kong, Macau or a compatriot of Taiwan do if he loses his travel certificate?

Task 3   Complete the following sentences by translating the Chinese in the brackets into English.

1. Passports are issued to the native people by _____ (外交部) .
2. She came here with a _____ (旅游签证).
3. A group of over 9 tourists can apply for a _____ (团体签证).
4. He was stopped by the police officer at the airport because his visa _____ (过期了).
5. A tour guide must know well about _____ (出入境条例).
6. Because he had too much currency, the money had to be _____ (向海关申报).
7. No entry for a person with _____ (犯罪记录).
8. On special occasions, _____ (落地签证) can be issued at the ports authorized by the Ministry of Public Security.

Case Study

Sophie is guiding a group on a "medical tour". The following day the group is taken to a resort where traditional Chinese medical treatments are offered. Many tourists experienced the treatments themselves and some purchased large quantities of herbal and other traditional medicine.

Questions

1. What do the tourists need to know when buying traditional Chinese medicine?
2. Which items are restricted by China's Customs?

1. 四大民间故事
2. 经典神话
3. 民俗大观——古代吉祥象征：四灵

Unit 11　Quintessence of Chinese Culture

▶▶ 导读

中华民族传统文化中有很多颇具代表性和富有独特内涵的文化遗产,如国画、京剧、中医等等。本单元选取其中三个独特精华:集益智性、趣味性、博弈性于一体的麻将,整体形态美与点画结构美并俱的书法,以及承载社会哲学、中医学、美学、气功、文化观念于一体的武术。

WARM-UP QUESTIONS

Have you ever practiced Chinese calligraphy or Chinese brush painting? Among all the Chinese opera forms, which one do you like best? Talk about them with your partners.

Unit 11 Quintessence of Chinese Culture

Text A

Chinese Calligraphy

Chinese calligraphy can be traced back to the inscriptions on bones, tortoise shells and bronzes on which the characters were carved with sharp angles. Later when there were the earliest books made up of bamboo pieces sewn together side by side, writing with brush came into being. The long history has thus witnessed the evolution of Chinese calligraphy and its various developed styles and schools.

Generally speaking, there are five categories of the scripts, namely the regular script (Kaishu), the running script (Xingshu), the cursive script (Caoshu), the clerical script (Lishu), and the seal script (Zhuanshu).① Running script and cursive script are less constrained and faster, where more movements made by the writing implement are visible. These styles' stroke orders vary more, sometimes creating radically different forms. They are descended from clerical script, in Han Dynasty as regular script, but running script and cursive script were used for personal notes only, and were never used as standard. Cursive script was highly appreciated during the reign of Emperor Wu of Han (140 BC—87BC).

Literally, the word "calligraphy" means beautiful writing. Chinese calligraphy is now universally acknowledged as one of the highest forms of Chinese visual art, serving the purpose of conveying thoughts in the meanwhile revealing the beauty of the characters. As the Chinese saying goes "A person's character is judged by the elegance of his handwriting"②, calligraphy mirrors a person's personalities, emotions, moral integrity, mindset, education background, achievement in self-cultivation, and aesthetic tastes.

Known as the "Four Treasures

Vocabulary

bronze 青铜器
sew 装订
evolution 进化
mindset 观念

of the Study"③, the writing brush, ink, paper and ink slab are the traditional writing implement in Chinese calligraphy. As a mental exercise, calligraphy coordinated the mind and body. Only through years of highly-disciplined practice can one master the shape, size, stretch and type of hair in the brush, the color and density of the ink, as well as the absorptive speed and surface texture of the paper.④ Wang Xizhi's *Foreword to Lanting Pavilion,* Yan Zhenqing's *Yan Qinli Tablet,* Liu Gongquan's *Xuanbi Pagoda Tablet,* together with Su Shi's *Book of Handwritten Poems* are all considered as the masterpieces of Chinese calligraphy.⑤

> ink slab 砚台
> contemporary 当代的

As the Chinese culture spread to Korea, Japan, Vietnam and Singapore, calligraphy has become a unique feature of oriental art. An increasing number of westerners have discovered the unique charm of Chinese calligraphy and have hence developed an interest in it. Picasso once said, "Had I been born Chinese, I would have been a calligrapher, not a painter." Today, the calligraphic tradition still remains alive in the work of many contemporary Chinese artists.

Notes

1. Generally speaking, there are five categories of the scripts, namely the regular script (Kaishu), the running script (Xingshu), the cursive script (Caoshu), the clerical script (Lishu), and the seal script (Zhuanshu). 书法大致分为五体,即楷书、行书、草书、隶属和篆书。
2. A person's character is judged by the elegance of his handwriting 字如其人
3. Four Treasures of the Study 文房四宝
4. Only through years of highly-disciplined practice can one master the shape, size, stretch and type of hair in the brush, the color and density of the ink, as well as the absorptive speed and surface texture of the paper. 只有经过多年的刻苦练习,才能掌握笔毛的形状、角度、位置、力度以及墨的颜色和浓度。
5. Wang Xizhi's *Foreword to Lanting Pavilion,* Yan Zhenqing's *Yan Qinli Tablet,* Liu Gongquan's *Xuanbi Pagoda Tablet,* together with Su Shi's *Book of Handwritten Poems* are all considered as the masterpieces of Chinese calligraphy. 王羲之的《兰亭序》、颜真卿的《颜勤礼碑》、柳公权的《玄秘塔碑》以及苏轼的《黄州寒食诗帖》被视为中国书法的杰出代表。

Unit 11 Quintessence of Chinese Culture

Text B

Wushu (Martial Arts)

Vocabulary

military 军事的
punching 打,击
thrusting 刺
defense 防御
immobility 不动,固定
external 外在的
temperament 气质,性情
coordinate 协调
routine 套路
pliability 柔韧性
suppleness 柔软性
leap 跳跃

Wushu, or Martial Arts, is a kind of Chinese traditional sport, as well as an important component of the cultural heritage of China, with a rich content over the centuries. Literally, "Wu" means "military", and "Shu" means "art".① Therefore, Wushu means the art of fighting, or martial arts. Martial training contains both series of actions and many single actions such as Ti (kicking), Da (punching), Shuai (throwing), Na (controlling), Ji (hitting) and Ci (thrusting).② Related to each style are basic forms, or sequences, which may involve defense strategies, offense, retreat, mobility and immobility, speed and slowness, hard or soft postures, emptiness and fullness, with or without weapons. Wushu, as a precious and varied culture, has a wide foundation among the mass population during its long history of social practice in China.③

The beginning of Chinese Wushu may date back to primitive society. At that time, in order to protect themselves and obtain food, men learned how to fight against the beasts using primitive tools like sticks as weapons. Later they made weapons in order to obtain food and goods from other people.④ So more weapons were made and the skills of fighting were also improved during the wars.

However, Wushu is by no means limited to the external movement. It also emphasizes on the full display of the internal temperament, mental attitude and potential of the human being.⑤ The practice of Wushu strengthens not only the bones and muscles, but also the internal organs and intelligence. It is essential to coordinate and cooperate with each and every movement of the hand, eye, body, foot and other parts of the body.

Wushu, therefore, can be taken as the basic exercise for other sporting activities. For example, the practice of the basic exercises and routines of Wushu is an effective way to improve the pliability of the joints and the suppleness of the back and legs.⑥ It can also help enhance human strength and

speed of movement by jumping and leaping and changes from one stance to another.⑦ In addition, the graceful movement of body, especially the typical oriental charm revealed during the exercises and practice of Wushu, not only has an impressive aesthetic effect, but also provides splendid visual delights.⑧ People can benefit mentally as well as physically from the display of Wushu offensive and defensive skills and the exertion of forces through their display.

aesthetic 美学的，审美的
offensive 进攻的
exertion 发挥，运用

Notes

1. Literally, "Wu" means "military", and "Shu" means "art". 从字面意思上讲，"武"意为"军事性的"，而"术"则为"艺术"。

2. Martial training contains both series of actions and many single actions such as Ti (kicking), Da (punching), Shuai (throwing), Na (controlling), Ji (hitting) and Ci (thrusting). 武术训练包括一系列的动作以及一些单独动作，譬如踢、打、摔、拿、击、刺。

3. Wushu, as a precious and varied culture, has a wide foundation among the mass population during its long history of social practice in China. 武术作为一种珍稀而又富于变化的文化，在中国民间有相当长的习武历史。

4. Later they made weapons in order to obtain foods and goods from other people. 后来，他们发明了更加具备杀伤性的武器来夺取他人的食物和财物。

5. It also emphasizes on the full display of the internal temperament, mental attitude and potential of the human being. 同时，武术强调内在性情、思想态度和人类潜能的完全展示。

6. For example, the practice of the basic exercises and routines of Wushu is an effective way to improve the pliability of the joints and the suppleness of the back and legs. 譬如，武术基本功和套路的练习能够有效地提高关节的柔韧性和背部、腿部的柔软伸展性。

7. It can also help enhance human strength and speed of movement by jumping and leaping and changes from one stance to another. 武术也能够通过跳跃和腾闪挪移来增强人体的力量加快动作的速度。

8. In addition, the graceful movement of the body, especially the typical oriental charm revealed during the exercises and practice of Wushu, not only has an impressive aesthetic effect, but also provides splendid visual delights. 除此之外，习武者身体的优美动作，特别是在习武中所体现出来的典型东方神韵，不仅会带来深刻的审美效果，而且还有壮观的视觉享受。

Unit 11 Quintessence of Chinese Culture

Text C

Mahjong

Vocabulary
tile 麻将牌
discard 丢弃,抛弃
bequeath 遗赠
benevolence 仁慈
filial 孝顺的
piety 虔诚

Mahjong, or Ma Que (sparrow), is a traditional Chinese game usually played by four people with the tiles drawn and discarded until one of the players wins with a hand of four combinations of three tiles and a pair of matching tiles. Unlike bridge or other card games, mahjong players do not play in teams; each player plays for himself.

When it comes to the origin of mahjong, some people believe that some soldiers during the Taiping Rebellion[①] created the game to kill time. Others believe that a Shanghai nobleman created the game in the 1870s. Still others say that two brothers from Ningbo created mahjong around 1850, from an earlier game called Ma Diao[②] (hanging horses).

Usually, a set of mahjong has 136 tiles, including bamboos, characters, circles, winds, and dragons while the 144-tile mahjong set has extra bonus tiles of seasons and flowers.[③] Bamboos, characters, circles are numbered from 1 to 9. Wind tiles are East, South, West and North. Dragon tiles are red middle, green prosperity and white board and they agree with the three virtues bequeathed by Confucius, namely benevolence, sincerity and filial piety.[④] There are four identical tiles for each of the bamboos, characters, circles, winds, and dragons.

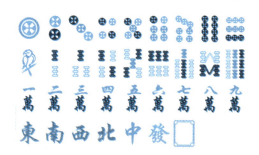

The rules of mahjong vary from region to region. Chinese classical mahjong, Hong Kong mahjong or Cantonese mahjong, Sichuan mahjong, Tianjin mahjong, Shenyang mahjong, Taiwanese mahjong are not only very popular games in China but also have a small following in western countries. In most variations, each player begins by receiving thirteen tiles. In turn players draw and discard tiles until they

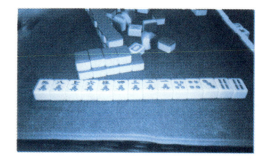

complete a winning hand. Typically, a winning hand consists of 14 tiles, made up of four melds (three identical tiles or three consecutive tiles of the same pattern) and a pair of two identical tiles.

Mahjong is more than just a game. In 2002, the first mahjong World Championship attracted players from China, Japan, Europe and the United States. The following years saw many more international mahjong tournaments and mahjong is now regarded as a sport.

meld 融合,组合
ingrain 根深蒂固
revive 使复原,振兴
moderately 适度地

The game has always been deeply ingrained in the Chinese community. However, it was banned by the government upon the founding of the People's Republic of China. The game was revived after "the Cultural Revolution"⑤. Today, the game has an extensive mass base as a leisure activity. Moderately playing mahjong is of great benefit to people's physical and mental health.

Notes

1. the Taiping Rebellion 太平天国运动
2. Ma Diao 马吊
3. Usually, a set of mahjong has 136 tiles, including bamboos, characters, circles, winds, and dragons while the 144-tile mahjong set has extra bonus tiles of seasons and flowers. 通常情况下，每副麻将牌有136张，花色包括条、万、饼、风和龙，而144张牌的麻将还包括季节和花牌。
4. Dragon tiles are red middle, green prosperity and white board and they agree with the three virtues bequeathed by Confucius, namely benevolence, sincerity and filial piety. 龙牌是红中、青发和白板，他们和儒家思想中的仁、义、孝正好对应。
5. "the Cultural Revolution" "文化大革命"

Useful Phrases and Expressions

1. come into being 形成
2. serve the purpose of... 以达到……目的
3. aesthetic taste 审美品位
4. be by no means limited to... 绝不仅限于
5. oriental charm 东方魅力

Unit 11 Quintessence of Chinese Culture

6. visual delight 视觉享受
7. kill time 打发时间
8. filial piety 孝道
9. more than just 不仅仅是
10. have extensive mass base 有广泛的群众基础

Exercises

Part I Listening Practice

Passage 1

Confucius Institute

platform 平台
exploration 探索
non-profit public institution 非盈利性公共机构
adapt to 适应
multitude 大量
enrollment 注册

Task 1 Listen to the passage carefully and then fill in the blanks with what you hear. The passage will be read only once.

Over recent years, the Confucius Institutes' development has been sharp and they have provided ____1____ for people all over the world to learn about Chinese language and culture. In addition they have become a ____2____ for cultural exchanges between China and the world as well as a bridge ____3____ friendship and cooperation between China and the rest of the world and are much welcomed across the globe.

As China's economy and exchanges with the world have seen rapid growth, there has also been a ____4____ increase in the world's demands for Chinese learning. ____5____ from the UK, France, Germany and Spain's experience in promoting their national languages, China began its own ____6____ through establishing non-profit public institutions which aim to promote Chinese language and culture in foreign countries in 2004: these were ____7____ the name Confucius Institute.

Confucius Institutes/Classrooms ____8____ flexible teaching patterns and adapt to suit local conditions when teaching Chinese language and promoting culture in foreign primary schools, ____9____ schools, communities and enterprises. In 2009, Confucius Institutes/Classrooms around the world offered 9,000 Chinese courses of a multitude of styles, with a total ____10____ of 260,000, a 130,000 strong enrollment increase from the previous year. More than 7,500 cultural exchange activities took place.

Task 2   Listen to the recording again and then answer the following questions.

(1) What is the importance of Confucius Institutes?

(2) Which countries did China learn from to promote the Chinese language?

(3) How did China begin its own exploration to promote the Chinese language?

(4) When did China start establishing non-profit institutions?

(5) How many courses were offered in Confucius Institutes/Classrooms in 2009?

Unit 11 Quintessence of Chinese Culture

Passage 2

Chinese Chess

strategist 战略家　　　　array 大批
finalize 最后确定　　　　highbrow 趣味高雅的人
lowbrow 文化艺术修养低的人　manual 手册，指南

Task 1 Listen to the passage carefully and then fill in the blanks with what you hear. The passage will be read only once.

Chinese chess has a long history. Its origin has not been confirmed yet. But judging by its rules, we can conclude that the origin of Chinese chess was closely related to _____1_____ strategists in ancient China.

During the Spring and Autumn Period and the Warring States Period, wars were fought for years on end. A new chess game was _____2_____ after the array of troops. This was the earliest form of Chinese chess.

During the Wei, Jin and Northern and Southern dynasties, a kind of chess game was popular among the people. It laid a foundation for the _____3_____ pattern of the Chinese chess.

In ancient times, the Chinese chess was always enjoyed by both highbrows and lowbrows.

During the _____4_____ of Suzong of the Tang Dynasty, Prime Minister Niu Sengru wrote a fake story about chess. That occurred during the Baoying period, so it was named Baoying chess. Baoying chess had six pieces. He wrote about the rules of the chess. Baoying chess produced a significant influence on the chess in _____5_____ years.

Three forms of chess took shape after the Song Dynasty. One of them consisted of 32 pieces. They were played on a chessboard with 9 _____6_____ lines and 9 horizontal lines. Popular in those days was a chessboard without a river _____7_____. The Chu River and Han Borderline were added later. This form has lasted to this day.

With the economic and cultural development during the Qing Dynasty, the Chinese chess entered a new stage. Many different schools of chess _____8_____ and chess players came into prominence. With the popularization of the Chinese chess, many books and _____9_____ on the techniques of playing chess were published.

They played an important role in _____10_____ the Chinese chess and improving the techniques of playing in modern times.

Task 2 Have you got a clear idea of the origin and development of the Chinese chess? Tell each other about the evolution of the Chinese chess without looking at the textbook.

Part II Oral Practice

Task 1 Group Discussion

Divide the class into small groups and each student will give his/her group member a summary of the quintessence of Chinese culture mentioned in the texts. Then ask other students to make some additions if necessary.

Task 2 Role Play

Work in groups of 4 or 5. One of you is a tour guide. The rest are foreign visitors who are very interested in mahjong, Wushu and the Chinese chess. The tour guide is going to introduce these parts of the quintessence of Chinese culture to them.

Part III Translation

Task 1 Translate the following words or phrases into English.

(1) 中华文明
(2) 文房四宝
(3) 琴棋书画
(4) 动静结合
(5) 增强体质
(6) 军事战略
(7) 赌博
(8) 世界锦标赛
(9) 心智挑战
(10) 内在性情

Unit 11 Quintessence of Chinese Culture

Task 2 Translate the following paragraph into English.

中国结艺是中国特有的民间手工编结艺术，它以其独特的东方神韵、丰富多彩的变化，充分体现了中国人民的智慧和深厚的文化底蕴。"中国结"就是绳结，为13个基本结。运用这13个基本结进行任意变化组合，就可以创造出无数美轮美奂的绳结工艺品。

Task 3 Translate the following paragraph into Chinese.

Modern designs may include your astrological sign (Eastern or Western), the flora or fauna of the seasons, or popular animation characters. Some stores are devoted exclusively to the sale of chopsticks. They offer various designs for eating foods ranging from needle sharp points for fish, to spiraled tips for spaghetti, to almost paddle-like ends for ochazuke (rice covered with green tea).

导游技巧和业务
Professional Tour Guiding Knowledge & Skills

货币知识

货币兑换 (currency exchange)
☞ 外汇政策
- 中国对外汇实行由国家"集中管理、统一经营"的方针。在中国境内，禁止外汇流通、使用、质押，禁止私自买卖外汇，禁止以任何形式进行套汇、炒汇、逃汇。
- 海外旅游者来华时携入的外汇和票据金额没有限制，但是数额大时须在入境时据实申报；
- 在中国境内，海外游客可持外汇到中国各银行兑换点兑换人民币；
- 兑换外币后，旅游者应妥善保管银行出具的外汇兑换证明 (exchange memo)(俗称"水单")，该证明有效期为6个月，旅游者若在半年内离开中国，兑换的人民币没有花完，可持护照和水单将其兑换成外币，但不得超过水单上注明的金额。

☞ 可兑换的外币
- 世界上有一百五十多种货币，在中国境内可兑换的外币有：美元 USD、欧元 EURO、英镑 GBP、日元 JPY、澳大利亚元 AUD、加拿大元 CAD、瑞士法郎 GHF、丹麦克朗 DKK、挪威克朗 NOK、瑞典克朗 SEK、新加坡元 SGD、港币 HKD、马来西亚林吉特 MYR、菲律宾比索 PHP、泰国铢 THB、韩元 KPW 和澳门元 MOP。我国台湾地区的新台币，可按内部牌价收兑。

旅行支票 (traveler's check)

☞ 概念
- 旅行支票是银行或旅行支票公司为方便旅游者，在旅游者交存一定金额后，签发的一种面额固定的、没有指定的付款人和付款地点的定额票据。
- 可以在世界各大城市、各大旅行社、各大饭店、各大百货公司当现金支付，可以在世界各大银行及发行商设立的兑换网点兑换现金或购买。

☞ 主要品种
- 现全球通行的旅游支票品种有：英国通济隆 (Thomas Cook)、巴克莱银行 (Barclays)、美国运通 (American Express)、美国花旗 (City Bank)、日本住友银行等发售的旅行支票。
- 除最为常用的美元旅行支票外，还有欧元、英镑、加元、澳元等币种的旅行支票。

☞ 注意事项
- 购买旅行支票时，购买者要当场签字，作为预留印鉴；支取款项时又须当着付款单位工作人员的面在支票上再次签字；付款单位将两个签字核对无误后方予付款，以防假冒。

信用卡

☞ 概念
- 信用卡是一种电子智能卡，卡上印有：发卡银行名称、持卡人姓名、卡号、有效期、预留签字、银行的简单申明等；
- 信用卡是银行或信用卡公司向客户提供小额消费信贷的一种信用凭证。

☞ 分类
- 按发卡机构，分为银行卡和非银行卡；
- 按持卡人的资信程度，分为普通卡、金卡和白金卡；

- 按偿清方式,分为贷记卡和借记卡;
  贷记卡(credit card):即"先消费,后还款",持卡人无须事先存款,就享有一定信贷额度的使用权;
  借记卡(debit card):即"先存款,后消费",持卡人必须先存款,按存款金额持卡消费,一般不允许透支。
  中国各银行发行的信用卡,多为借记卡。
- 按流通范围,分为国际卡和地区卡。
  我国目前受理的主要外国信用卡有7种:万事达卡(MASTER CARD)、维萨卡(VISA CARD)、运通卡(AMERICAN EXPRESS)、大莱卡(DINERS CARD)、JCB卡(JCB CARD)、百万卡(MILLION CARD)和发达卡(FEDERAL CARD)。
  我国公民出境旅游,应尽量使用信用卡,既安全又省去许多麻烦。

小贴士

旅行支票与银行卡相比,有哪些优点?

◇ 方便
  旅行支票可以当现金支付。旅行支票面额齐全,如美元旅行支票最大面值为1000美元,最小面值为20美元;
  旅行支票可以在世界各大银行、兑换网点兑换现金;而银行卡必须是在开户银行的境外分行或代理行兑换当地货币。

◇ 实惠
  旅行支票在银行兑现,手续费更低;在国际饭店等消费场所直接付款,无须支付任何费用。一些发行机构,如美国运通,在世界各大城市还设立了免费兑付网点,如我国的北京、上海。

Discussion & Exercise

Task 1 Can anyone purchase goods in China's shopping centers with foreign currencies?

Task 2 What is traveler's check? When accepting traveler's checks, what should you pay attention to?

Task 3 Complete the following sentences by translating the Chinese contained in the brackets into English.

1. He made his payment _____ (用信用卡).
2. Restrictions on _____ (外汇) will soon be lifted.
3. Do you accept _____ (旅行支票).
4. There's 4% _____ (贸易商委托费).
5. We honor Master Card, Diner's Card, Visa, Federal Card, and _____ (美国运通卡)?
6. What is the _____ (兑换率) between the British Pound and RMB?
7. The cashier must check and see if the credit card is still _____ (有效).
8. Please keep this _____ (水单/兑换单), since you may need it when you wish to change it back to your own currency.

Sophie received a Spanish tour group comprising mostly women. One of the women is very interested in a silk cheongsam, and wants to exchange some Spanish currency with Sophie because she doesn't have enough Chinese Yuan to pay for it.

Questions

1. What should Sophie do when the tourist wants to exchange currency with her?
2. What should tourists be informed regarding currency exchange?

1. 魅力汉字
2. 国画鉴赏
3. 民俗大观——武术文化

Unit 12　Special Interest Tourism

▶▶ 导读

> 孔子曰:"知之者不如好之者,好之者不如乐之者。"当旅游携手兴趣,将成就如何动人的景致和绚丽的心情?时下,摆脱传统的旅游思维模式,选择自己感兴趣的线路踏上一段旅途、满足特殊兴趣的个性化旅游日益成为人们新的选择。

WARM-UP QUESTIONS

What hobbies do you have? Have you ever taken a tour to satisfy one of your personal interests? What types of special interest tourism do you know? Talk about it with your partner.

实用导游英语

Text A

Tours by Interest

Special interest tourism is one of the fastest growing segments, with an ever increasing range of specializations found in product supply.① A more mature travelling public is increasingly seeking experiences which satisfy a whole spectrum of interests. Accordingly, there is a need for new tourism products, services and experiences that cater to these special needs. China is blessed with a diversity of resources for the development of special interest tourism. It has gained popularity among tourists who are seeking individualized holiday experience.

Vocabulary

segment 部分，细分市场
quintessence 精髓
spectrum 系列
culinary 烹饪的，美食的
enticing 迷人的，诱人的
venue 场所，场馆
gourmet 美食，美食家
plantation 种植园

Some of special interest tours in China along with a short description for them are:

China Kung Fu Tours   An interesting Kung Fu trip will make a fan's Kung Fu dream come true. Wudang Mountains and Shaolin Temple are the Meccas of Chinese martial arts②.

There travelers can truly understand the quintessence of Chinese Kung Fu culture. Tourists watch stunning Kungfu performances by Kungfu masters or even participate in the training courses to learn Kungfu.

China Culinary Tours   Enticing cuisine culture comes to life when you experience the first-hand local dishes and specialties.③ A China gourmet tour will cover the most popular destinations blended with the typical Chinese cuisines. On a culinary trip, tourists have the chance to dine in a variety of venues, probably at private clubs, gourmet restaurants or private homes. In addition to local cuisine tasting, opportunities are also given to enjoy cooking lessons and practice cooking skills.

China Tea Tours   Led by professional travel guides, tourists explore mist-covered mountains and plantations to discover the mysterious lure of tea. On a

Unit 12 Special Interest Tourism

tour in the destinations of tea production, tourists experience diversified traditions saturated with tea elements.④ A tea culture tour usually includes picking up tea leaves under the guidance of local farmers, enjoying the varied processes of making tea products and a traditional art—tea ceremony performance which showcases the rich content of tea culture.

saturate 渗透, 包含

China Panda Tours Panda tours are arranged to visit the panda reserves and provide the rare opportunity for travelers to see the lovely pandas in person, hug them, feed them or even join a volunteer program to take care of them. To take a panda reserve base volunteer tour is an once-in-a-lifetime experience. It is the best opportunity to get closer to the China's national treasure. Bifengxia Panda Reserve Base⑤ is world's largest panda reserve base. Here, wearing special working clothes, you will be a panda keeper to feed the cute pandas, clean their house, help the panda take a cool path, watch and learn some interesting facts about them.

Notes

1. Special interest tourism is one of the fastest growing segments, with an ever increasing range of specializations found in product. 特殊兴趣旅游是旅游行业增长最快的细分市场之一，提供越来越多的个性化产品。
2. the Meccas of Chinese martial arts 中国武术的圣地/发源地
3. Enticing cuisine culture comes to life when you experience the first-hand local dishes and specialties. 当亲自品尝地道的地方菜肴和特产时，绝妙诱人的饮食文化就变得生动鲜活。
4. On a tour in the destinations of tea production, tourists experience diversified traditions saturated with tea elements. 在茶产地畅游，游客可以体验渗透着茶文化的多姿多彩的传统。
5. Bifengxia Panda Reserve Base 碧峰峡熊猫保护基地

Text B

Adventure Tourism

Adventure tourism seeks to provide experiences beyond one's normal comfort zone. It can be a tour designed around an adventurous activity. The activities can be physically challenging, but can also expand cultural and spiritual boundaries. Although adventure tourism means different things to different people, it is generally defined as a type of travel in an unusual, exotic, remote or wilderness setting and often involves different levels of risks, difficulties and physical activities.①

Adventure tourism covers a wide variety of vacations, but all are activity-based. Mountaineering, trekking, bungee jumping, mountain biking, rafting, zip-lining, paragliding, bushwalking, climbing, abseiling, kayaking, caving, ballooning, diving, off-road driving and many similar activities forms the basis for adventure tourism.② Adventure tourism can range from "getting wet" such as whitewater rafting, to "getting high" such as paragliding, to "getting faster" such as zorbing.

The broad idea of adventure tourism is also broken into two major subcategories of adventure tourism: hard adventure and soft adventure.③ Hard adventure tourism generally involves an element of physical danger or risk. Soft adventure tourism simply seeks to explore areas that are not typical for travelers, such as visiting relatively undeveloped destinations for new experiences, activities, cultures, and natural wonders. It involves less risk and some mild physical activity.

Thrill tourism is the best known type of hard adventure tourism. Bungee jumping, whitewater rafting, mountaineering, parasailing, rock climbing and spelunking are all popular forms of thrill tourism. Ethno tourism is a form of soft tourism that brings participants into contact with local cultures and diverse indigenous people around the globe. It is often in the form of long treks into undeveloped areas with a certain amount of

Vocabulary

adventurous 冒险性的
exotic 奇异的,异国情调的
wilderness 荒野
whitewater rafting 漂流
zorbing 太空球
parasailing 水上滑翔运动
spelunking 洞穴探险
indigenous 土著的
trek 长途徒步

risk.

Along with the swift development of China's economy, people who are getting richer by the day can now afford the big expenses of adventure tourism. A new trend of participating in adventure tourism has been grabbing the attention of Chinese tourists. Some routes of adventure tourism are well-designed and promoted by travel agencies and local tourism administrations. Adventure routes like the Ancient Cliff tour ④ and the Takla Makan Desert ⑤ tour are attractive to a soaring number of tourists who are finding joy through unfamiliar, mysterious and breathtaking experiences.

breathtaking 惊险刺激的

Notes

1. Although adventure tourism means different things to many people, it is generally defined as a type of travel that will be done in an unusual, exotic, remote or wilderness setting and often involves low or high levels of risks, difficulties and physical activities. 虽然人们对探险旅游的理解不同，但一般来讲探险旅游被定义为这样的旅行：到一个不熟悉、奇异偏远的地方或者荒僻野外，通常会有一定程度的危险、艰难和包括一定强度的体力活动。

2. Mountaineering, trekking, bungee jumping, mountain biking, rafting, zip-lining, paragliding, bushwalking, climbing, abseiling, kayaking, caving, ballooning, diving, off-road driving and many similar activities forms the basis for adventure tourism. 探险旅游指的是登山、徒步远足、蹦极、山地自行车、漂流、高空滑索、滑翔、丛林徒步、攀爬、沿绳滑降、划皮艇、洞穴探险、热气球运动、潜水、越野驾驶等之类的活动。这些活动构成探险旅游的基础。

3. hard adventure and soft adventure 硬探险旅游和软探险旅游。根据探险旅游的危险性、冒险性程度以及旅游者探险经验和技能熟练的程度，探险旅游可以分为硬探险旅游和软探险旅游。软探险旅游对旅游者体力要求不高，危险性或冒险性大都可以人为控制，如野营探险旅游、土著民俗旅游等。进行硬探险旅游时，冒险性较大，不可预知性强，对旅游者的探险经历、探险技能、专业水平、探险装备等要求较高，如漂流探险旅游、沙漠探险旅游等。

4. the Ancient Cliff tour 古崖探险游

5. the Takla Makan Desert tour 塔克拉玛干沙漠之旅

Text C

Photography Tourism

Everyone gets a bit snap-happy on holiday, but for some, taking photographs is the reason to travel in the first place. Whether you're an amateur or professional snapper, photography tours are designed with photo-taking first and foremost in mind. It ranges from wildlife photography holidays to cultural trips, so you can capture everything from landscapes and locals to the hustle and bustle of daily life.①

As a sub category of special interest tourism, photography tourism has evolved out of specific interest or hobby of taking photographs. The whole purpose of a photographic tour is geared around the specific need to take photographs. Usually, people with a shared interest in photography come together to have a friendly, exciting and unforgettable trip, be it to the dramatic Arctic②, the indescribable Antarctic③, the fantastic Galapagos Islands④, or other far-flung regions of our wonderful planet. Photography tours also provide a great opportunity to improve one's photographic skills and overall knowledge of landscapes, wildlife and culture.

There are photographic tours of various types. It can be a photo cruise tour, a wildlife photographic expedition or guided photo-shootings of landscapes, flora, attractions and people. Some tours are unique in that they combine photographic opportunities at selected destinations with technical courses and photographic workshops. They cover subjects as diverse as photographic analysis and historical and anthropological issues.⑤ Companies specializing in photographic tours focus on services unique to the holiday. They include professional photographers as team leaders or as "resident experts" accompanying the tour.⑥

From its gorgeous landscapes to its unique culture, China offers endless opportunities for amateur and professional photographers alike to take perfect photos. There are many popular photography destinations and attractions, including the amazing terraced rice fields⑦ and idyllic Yangshuo County in picturesque Guilin, the pure and mysterious land of

Vocabulary

snap 照片,拍照
amateur 业余的
capture 拍摄,捕捉
indescribable 难以形容的,无法描述的
far-flung 偏远的
expedition 远征,探险
flora 植物群落
anthropological 人类学的
resident 驻留的
gorgeous 美丽壮观的

Unit 12 Special Interest Tourism

Tibet, the legendary Shangri-La in Yunnan, the fairyland Jiuzhaigou, and the most magnificent mountain Huangshan. On these unbelievable photography tours in China, tourists appreciate not only the amazing natural wonders that China has to offer, but also the welcoming local people, as well as their cultures and traditions.

Notes

1. Whether you're an amateur or professional snapper, photography tours are designed with photo-taking first and foremost in mind. It includes wildlife photography holidays to cultural trips, so you can capture everything from landscapes and locals to the hustle and bustle of daily life. 不论你是业余还是专业的摄影爱好者，拍照是设计摄影旅游时首先要考虑的。这类旅游不仅包括野生动物摄影之旅也有文化摄影旅游，因此你可以捕捉到各种题材，从多彩风景、土著居民到日常生活的熙来攘往。

2. Arctic 北冰洋

3. Antarctic 南极

4. Galapagos Islands 加拉帕戈斯群岛：又名科隆群岛，隶属厄瓜多尔，以其保持原始风貌的独特生物物种而闻名于世，素有"生物进化活博物馆"之称，1979年被列入世界遗产名录。为了保护群岛的自然环境，每年只允许一万名游客进入。加拉帕戈斯群岛还吸引了大批自然爱好者及水下呼吸管、戴水肺潜水爱好者。这个地方是世界上七大潜水胜地之首。

5. Some tours are unique in that they combine photographic opportunities at selected destinations with technical courses and photographic workshops covering subjects as diverse as photographic analysis and historical and anthropological issues. 有些摄影旅行独具一格，它们将精心挑选的摄影目的地与摄影技术课程和专题研讨会集合起来。研讨会涵盖的主题广泛，不仅包括摄影分析，也会讨论历史及人类学各种议题。

6. Companies specializing in photographic tours focus on services unique to the holiday. They include professional photographers as team leaders or as "resident experts" accompanying the tour. 专业从事摄影旅游的公司强调提供独一无二的服务，如安排专业摄影师作为领队或驻队专家全程陪同。

7. terraced rice fields 水稻梯田

实用导游英语

Useful Phrases and Expressions

1. expand cultural and spiritual boundaries 丰富文化知识，陶冶情操
2. be broken into ... categories 分为……类
3. in the form of 以……的形式
4. bring...into contact with 使接触到，使体验
5. grab the attention of 吸引……的注意力
6. first and foremost 首先，首要的是
7. evolve out of 从……逐渐发展成，源于
8. the hustle and bustle 喧嚣，喧闹，熙熙攘攘
9. specialize in 专门经营，专业从事
10. cater to 满足，迎合
11. gain popularity 深受欢迎，日益普遍
12. an once-in-a-lifetime experience 一生只有一次的经历

Exercises

Part I Listening Practice

Passage 1

Adventure Tourism Gains Popularity

sight-seeing attractions 观光胜地
reveler 狂欢者
acrobat 杂技，特技演员
bring history alive 鲜活再现历史

opt to do 选择做……
hoist up 举起，抬起
kick 极大的兴奋、刺激和乐趣

Unit 12 Special Interest Tourism

Task 1 Listen to the passage carefully and then fill in the blanks with what you hear. The passage will be read only once.

It's the middle of the golden week holiday. And while most tourists have ___1___ a visit or two to some well-known sight-seeing attractions, more and more people are ___2___ to take less crowded, but more "___3___" excursions.

At the ancient city of "Tangwang" in eastern China's Shandong Province, revelers are really putting the "___4___" in holiday activities. They're recreating a battle that took place 1,400 years ago, during the Tang Dynasty. The show is ___5___ by dozens of acrobats, and attracts thousands of tourists each day. But the really exciting part is when the show ends—and people are ___6___ to ride the horses across the battlefield.

Or they can be hoisted up to be kung-fu super heroes, if they ___7___.

Li Zhiwen, a tourist from Beijing, said, "As a big fan of Chinese Kungfu novels, I've long dreamt of being able to fly. I ___8___ my dream here today. It's so cool!"

Sun Tingting, a tourist from Shanghai, said, "I like the show. It brings history ___9___. In one moment, I thought I'd gone back in time, and was back in the Tang Dynasty."

As tourism in China develops, there seems to be ever more ways for adventure hungry tourists to get their kicks. A strong trend is ___10___ to "experience"—rather than just "see" history.

Task 2 Listen to the recording again and then answer the following questions.

(1) What tours are increasingly popular in the golden week holiday?
_____

(2) What is the really exciting part of the show in the city of "Tangwang"?
_____

(3) Who performed the show to attract tourists?
_____

(4) Why does Sun Tingting, a tourist from Shanghai, like the show?
_____

(5) What is the strong trend for the tourism in China?
_____

Passage 2

Special Interest Tourism

> niche markets 利基市场
> trek (徒步)艰难旅行，跋涉，远足
> propose 提出（理论或解释）
> outback Australia 澳大利亚内陆
> dedicated 热衷的，投入的
> customized 量身定制的
> engage with 从事
> sample 品尝

Task 1 Listen to the passage carefully and then fill in the blanks with what you hear. The passage will be read only once.

Special interest tourism (SIT) is defined as travelling with the ___1___ of practising or enjoying a special interest. This can include unusual hobbies, activities, themes or destinations, which tend to attract niche markets. The term "special interest tourism" has traditionally been used for those ___2___ which focus on activities to attract a small number of highly dedicated visitors. These may be relatively unusual hobbies or activities which are practised by only a few people.

Douglas describes special interest tourism as an alternative to ___3___. It is the provision of customized tourism activities that ___4___ the specific interests of groups and individuals. In this case, tourism is ___5___ to satisfy a particular interest or need. Most special interest tours provide an expert tour leader and usually visit places and/or events only ___6___ to that interest.

It has been proposed that SIT ___7___ four main experiences: rewarding, enriching, adventuresome experiences, learning experiences. Clients engaged with SIT are seeking to learn more, enrich their awareness, and express themselves. They expect high standards of service and ___8___ focus.

The range of special interest tours is enormous. It may ___9___ a women's only trek down the Larapinta Track in outback Australia to a bike tour of one of French wine growing regions where it is possible to meet those responsible for the production of the wine being sampled, or from gay-only _____10_____ to whale watching in Antarctica.

Task 2　Have you got a clearer idea of special interest tourism? Share your understanding of this type of tourism with each other.

Part II Oral Practice

Task 1　Group Discussion

　　Divide the class into small groups and students in the group discuss the type of special interest tourism that they like and what they like about it. Then choose one representative from each group to report his/her ideas to the class.

Task 2　Role Play

　　Work in groups of 5 or 6. One of you is a clerk working for an international travel agency specializing in special interest tourism. The rest are foreign visitors. The clerk interviews the visitors to find out their special interests. Based on the findings, the clerk designs a special interest tour for the visitors and gives a detailed description of the tour.

Part III Translation

Task 1　Translate the following words or phrases into English.

(1) 漂流
(2) 土著
(3) 地方旅游局
(4) 野生动物奇观
(5) 梯田
(6) 风景如画的桂林
(7) 国内外
(8) 地方特产
(9) 神秘魅力
(10) 文化精髓

实用导游英语

 Task 2　Translate the following paragraph into English.

　　自行车旅行一般指的是自给自足的远途自行车骑行,首要追求乐趣、冒险和自主而不是运动、通勤或锻炼。自行车旅行可以由参加者自行规划和组织,也可以由专业旅行公司或俱乐部组团进行。自行车旅行可在任何时间进行,骑行距离也变化很大。根据身体状况、速度和停靠的次数,骑手一般一天可骑行50—150公里。几天的短途骑行的距离可能只有200公里,一次长途骑行可以穿越整个国家或周游世界。

 Task 3　Translate the following paragraph into Chinese.

　　In short, backpacking can be described as an independent, often international, low-budget way of travelling. Backpacking includes the use of a backpack or other luggage that is easily carried for long distances or long periods of time and inexpensive lodging such as youth hostels. It is typically associated with youth who generally have few obligations and thus more time to travel. Someone who backpacks is called a "Backpacker". Backpackers generally travel for a longer period of time than most other tourists, and they tend to travel in several different countries to meet locals as well as seeing the sights.

导游技巧和业务
Professional Tour Guiding Knowledge & Skills

跨文化意识

非言语交际 (non-verbal communication)
☞ 目光语
- 在与外国游客交流过程中,要与游客有目光交流,但也不能目不转睛地盯着对方,尤其是异性,否则会使对方反感。

☞ 表情语
- 与外国游客交流过程中,要灵活运用表情语,以利于情感的确切传达。

☞ 手势语
- 各民族都用手势表达一定的意义,但同一手势在不同的文化中可能有着不同的含义。因此在接待不同国家、不同地区的旅游者时,导游要准确、恰当地运用手势语。

- 按国际礼仪,为表示尊重,传递物品要用双手,但是在伊斯兰国家,人们认为左手不干净,不用左手传递物品或吃东西。

☞ 身势语
- 一般来说,南欧、中东、拉丁美洲地区的人们讲话时动作较多,动作幅度也较大;北欧、英美、亚洲人动作较少,幅度也较小。

☞ 方位语
- 来自不同文化背景的人,在进行言语交流时,保持一定的空间与距离有其内在的涵义,人们所接受的舒适距离不一样。影响人际距离的因素很多,包括性别、年龄、关系远近和文化背景等。

禁忌 (taboo)

☞ 隐私方面
- 不能直接问外国游客的年龄、收入、体重、婚姻状况、宗教信仰等。

☞ 语言歧视方面
- 避免使用涉及性别、年龄、身体缺陷、种族或名族歧视的语言。

☞ 饮食方面
- 外国人忌讳动物的头脚、内脏和血液,如糖醋活鲤鱼、甲鱼、乳鸽等。

☞ 数字方面
- 西方人比较喜欢3和7,信仰基督教的人士特别忌讳13和星期五,认为这一数字和日期是厄运和灾难的象征。

☞ 颜色方面
- 新加坡人忌讳黑色和红色、德国人忌讳墨绿色、法国人忌讳黄色、欧美许多国家人忌讳黑色。

社会交往

☞ 表达方式
- 东方人的情感表达间接、含蓄;
- 西方人的情感表达则直接、外露。

☞ 恭维与谦虚 (compliment and modesty)
- 对于对方的赞扬,中国人常表现出谦虚,委婉拒绝别人的恭维,尽量贬低自己;
- 西方人则欣然接受对方的赞扬,往往表现出高兴与感激。

☞ 送礼物
- 中国人在送礼时,比较重视礼物的价值,一般来说,对方的社会地位越高,礼品就要越贵重;西方人一般更重视礼品包含的意义,并避免赠送贵重的礼物,以免被误会为贿赂。
- 中国人在受礼时往往需要一再推辞，且在客人面前不打开礼物；西方国家受礼人一般不推辞，接受礼物后会即刻表示感谢，并当面拆开，不论其价值大小，都会对礼物表示赞赏。

> **小贴士**
>
> **如何向外国游客送礼？**
> - 选择具有中国特色的礼物：如风筝、二胡、笛子、剪纸、图章、脸谱、书画、文房四宝、茶叶、瓷瓶、唐三彩、织锦、香木扇、中国结、民俗手工艺品、中国特色的人偶摆件等。
> - 注重包装：西方人在送礼时十分看重礼品的包装，使其包装尽善尽美，忌讳用白色、棕色或黑色的纸包装礼品；多数国家的人们习惯用彩色包装纸或丝带包装，西欧国家喜欢用淡色包装纸。包装纸上不要有忌讳的花卉、动物图案。
> - 介绍礼品，不要过谦：向外国友人赠送礼品时，既要说明其寓意、特点与用途，又要说明它是为对方精心选择的，不要说过谦的话。

Discussion & Exercise

Task 1　What kinds of intercultural communication barriers can occur when you talk to your foreign tourists?

Task 2　How can we effectively overcome intercultural communication barriers?

Task 3　Complete the following sentences by translating the Chinese in the brackets into English.

1. Some normally acceptable rules of _____ (礼仪) may be considered inappropriate or even impolite on some occasions.
2. Americans tend to _____ (接受赞扬) while Chinese generally murmur some reply about not being worthy of the praise.
3. Dragon has different connotations in Chinese and western cultures. In Chinese culture, dragon is an _____ (吉祥的动物) that supposedly brings good luck, while to westerners it is often a symbol of evil and a fierce monster.
4. Red is a very lucky and festive color in Chinese culture. It is often associated with _____ (庆祝活动和喜庆日子). In western eyes, however, red often connotes

blood, revolution, and violence.

5. _____ (禁忌) refers to prohibition of a set of behaviours that should be avoided because they are offensive and impolite.
6. A _____ (委婉语) is the substitution of an agreeable or less offensive and disturbing expression.
7. Americans tend to use a _____ (直截了当的) form of request whereas Chinese tend to ask for a favor in a more roundabout and implicit way.
8. All _____ (身势语) should be interpreted within a given context; otherwise, it may be misleading.

Case Study

Travel agencies often give small gifts to foreign tourists, but inappropriate gifts might be considered rude. For example, it is inappropriate to give a handkerchief, a rose or a cowhide wallet to an Italian, Japanese or Indian. They need to pay attention to the color and pattern of the wrapping as well, and avoid saying "It's nothing. I hope you won't reject it."

Questions
1. In this case, why are the gifts not appropriate? What gifts should not be given?
2. How to choose appropriate gifts for foreigners?

1. 新旅游,新生活
2. 朝鲜风,边境游
3. 民俗大观——陶瓷

Unit 13　Emerging Tourism

▶▶ 导读

> 旅游新兴业态是传统旅游业升级和多元化发展的新兴领域,其文化内容更丰富,形式更多样。在中国,红色旅游让您瞻仰革命圣地,重温烽火岁月;乡村旅游让您远离尘嚣,品领民俗风情,寻心灵一份静谧安宁;养生旅游让您修身养性,回归自然,体验天人合一。

WARM-UP QUESTIONS

What do you know about the following scenic spots and traditional Chinese medicine? Discuss with your partners.

Unit 13 Emerging Tourism

Text A

Red Tourism

Red tourism, also known as revolutionary tourism, is a subset of tourism in China in which Chinese people visit revolutionary sites with historical significance so as to rekindle a long-lost sense of class struggle and proletarian principles①. It is a new tourism product which combines patriotic education with the tourism industry.

With ever increasing cultural richness, contemporary red tourism covers the revolutionary and development history of modern China from the founding of the Communist Party of China (CPC) in 1921 to present. In China, the five destinations most associated with red tourism are Yan'an, Shaoshan, Nanchang, Jinggang Mountain and Zunyi.

Yan'an, located in northern Shaanxi Province, is regarded as the holy land of CPC revolution. Being near the endpoint of the Long March②, it became the center of the Chinese Communist Revolution from 1935 to 1948. Moreover, Chinese Communists celebrate Yan'an as the birthplace of the revolution. Today tourists in Yan'an can participate in daily mock battles portraying the "The Defense of Yan'an"③ against Chinese nationalist army forces.

Vocabulary

subset 分组，子集
rekindle 重新点燃
proletarian 无产阶级的
patriotic 爱国的
contemporary 当代的
mock 模拟的
boost 促进，提高

Shaoshan, situated in Hunan Province, is the hometown of Mao Zedong. Mao's legend has boosted tourism in Shaoshan. There are seven tourist areas encompassing 82 tourist spots. The most popular sights are the Former Residence of Chairman Mao, Memorial Hall of Mao, Bronze Statue of Mao, Stone Tablets of Mao's Poems, and the Mao Memorial Garden.④

Nanchang is the capital city of Jiangxi Province. It is considered as a heroic city in China, in that it was the site of a significant uprising: August 1, 1927 Nanchang Uprising⑤, which was led by Zhou Enlai and He Long. In Nanchang City, there are many well-preserved historical sites of the uprising, including the General Headquarters of the Uprising,

He Long's Headquarters, and the New Fourth Army Headquarters.⑥

  Jinggang Mountain, located in Jiangxi Province, is celebrated as the cradle of the Chinese Communist Revolution and Red Army's birthplace, where Mao Zedong and other members of CPC, in 1927, established the first rural base of the revolution. Famous red historical sites located in Jinggang Mountain are the Former Residence of Mao Zedong, the First Hospital of China's Red Army, Joining Forces Memorial Hall and Revolutionary Martyrs Cemetery.⑦

  Zunyi, situated in Guizhou Province, is famous for the site of Zunyi Conference⑧. The Zunyi Conference was held in 1935, during the Long March. It was during this conference that Mao Zedong was elected as the leader of CPC for the first time.

  "Red culture" has become a major driving force behind the sustainable development of red tourism. The perfect combination of red culture and the experience economy has enabled red tourism to take on diverse forms such as "red themed" sight-seeing, education, restaurants, leisure, experiences, art, performances, exhibitions, and business.

  The significance of expanding red tourism lies in that it will benefit the inheritance of advanced culture and traditional spirit of the Chinese nation. It helps to make red tourism more consistent with the times and reality, further explore valuable spiritual wealth of red tourism and enrich the essence of red tourism.

> martyr 烈士
> cemetery 墓地,公墓
> inheritance 继承

Notes

1. so as to rekindle a long-lost sense of class struggle and proletarian principles 以重温阶级斗争的烽火岁月和无产阶级的革命精神
2. Long March 长征。1934年10月,中央主力红军为摆脱国民党军队的围剿,被迫实行战略大转移,退出根据地进行长征。经过12个省,翻越18座山脉,渡过24条河流,行程约两万五千里,于1935年10月到达陕北,与陕北红军胜利会师。
3. The Defense of Yan'an 延安保卫战
4. The most popular sights are the Former Residence of Chairman Mao, Memorial Hall of Mao, Bronze Statue of Mao, Stone Tablets of Mao's Poems, and the Mao Memorial Garden.著名的景点有:毛泽东故居、毛泽东纪念馆、毛泽东铜像、毛泽东诗词碑林和毛泽东纪念园等。
5. August 1, 1927, Nanchang Uprising 八一南昌起义,简称"南昌起义"或"八一起义"。1927年8月1日,由周恩来、贺龙等领导的中国共产党势力的军队针对国民党的分共政策,发起武装反抗。
6. including the General Headquarters of the Uprising, He Long's Headquarters, and the New Fourth Army Headquarters 有南昌起义总指挥部旧址、贺龙指挥部旧址和南昌新四军军部旧址等
7. Famous red historical sites located in Jinggang Mountain are the Former Residence of Mao Zedong, the First Hospital of China's Red Army, Joining Forces Memorial Hall and Revolutionary Martyrs

Cemetery. 井冈山的著名红色景点有：毛泽东旧居、小井红军医院、井冈山会师纪念馆和井冈山革命烈士陵园等。

8. Zunyi Conference 遵义会议。1935年1月15—17日，中共中央政治局在贵州遵义，召开了独立自主地解决中国革命问题的一次极其重要的扩大会议。此次会议，确立了毛泽东在党和军队中的领导地位。

Text B

Rural Tourism

Rural tourism, regarded as "country experience", has become an increasingly popular lifestyle in China. It involves travelers in visiting destinations in agricultural or non-urban areas and experiencing elements of traditional life.

According to the diversity of destinations, rural tourism in China can generally be classified into three types: culture-based rural tourism, nature-based rural tourism and agro-tourism.

Culture-based rural tourism refers to leisure travel for the purpose of experiencing the place and activities that represent the past, such as the folk custom villages and ancient towns in China①. Top destinations for this type of tourism are the ancient towns and villages in China where traditional architecture, lifestyle, folklore and crafts are well preserved. Zhouzhuang, Wuzhen and Zhujiajiao are representatives of beautiful South China water towns. Picturesque scenery, quaint bridges and ancient dwellings along the river deliver a peaceful feeling to visitors.② One can learn more about Hui-style architecture by visiting Hongcun and Xidi at the foot of Mountain Huangshan. Moreover, ancient villages and towns in southwest China, such as the Lijiang ancient town in Yunnan, are ideal places to experience the traditional lifestyle of ethnic minorities.

Nature-based rural tourism, also referred to as recreation-based tourism, alludes to the visitation of natural scenic areas. Such areas include those mountains, rivers, lakes and forests that are abundant with plant and animal wildlife. Here, tourists can appreciate beautiful natural scenes or take part in outdoor recreation/adventure activities, such as angling, climbing and horse riding. Wuyuan in Jiangxi is known as "the most beautiful

Vocabulary

agro-tourism 农业旅游
quaint 古色古香的
dwelling 住宅，住处
allude 暗指，提及
angling 钓鱼

rapeseed 油菜,油菜籽
pastoral 田园般的
orchard 果园
ranch 牧场,农场
transition 转变
upgrading 升级

countryside" in China, and the blossoming of rapeseed flowers is one of the greatest tourist attractions③. Every spring, tens of thousands of visitors swam into the villages to marvel at its beauty.

The third major category of rural tourism is agro-tourism, commonly known as "Happy Farmhouse Tourism" or "Farm Stay", which refers to the act of visiting a farm or any agricultural or horticultural operation for the purpose of enjoyment, education or engagement in rural life. The "agro-entertainment" approach to leisure time not only offers opportunities to enjoy pastoral scenery, but also a hands-on experience of farm life,④ including fruit picking in the orchard, harvesting vegetables in the field, barbecue, engaging in overnight farm or ranch stays, and visiting agriculture-related festivals and museums. Chengdu was named the "Birthplace of Happy Farmhouse Tourism" by the National Tourism Administration at the opening ceremony of the first China Rural Tourism Festival in 2006.⑤ As more and more urban travelers seek an escape from the hustle and bustle of the city, agri-tourism has grown in popularity in China.

In recent years, rural tourism has witnessed rapid development. Developing tourism in rural areas can serve as a new way to promote rural economy. Rural tourism has already become an important engine to pass down ancient culture, enrich peasants and promote rural economic transition and upgrading.⑥

Notes

1. such as the folk custom villages and ancient towns in China 如中国的民俗村、古村镇等
2. Picturesque scenery, quaint bridges and ancient dwellings along the river deliver a peaceful feeling to visitors. 小桥、流水、石巷、老屋,如诗如画的江南古镇,成为游客远离尘嚣的又一世外桃源。
3. the blossoming of rapeseed flowers is one of the greatest tourist attractions 片片金黄的油菜花田,是婺源的一大景点
4. The "agro-entertainment" approach to leisure time not only offers pastoral scenery, but also a hands-on experience of farm life... 这种将传统农业与娱乐休闲相结合的新型旅游,让游客不仅可以欣赏到优美的田园风光,同样也可以亲身体验田园生活……
5. Chengdu was named the "Birthplace of Happy Farmhouse Tourism" by the National Tourism Administration at the opening ceremony of the first China Rural Tourism Festival in 2006. 在2006年中国首届乡村旅游节开幕式上,国家旅游局授予成都"中国农家乐旅游发源地"称号。
6. Rural tourism has already become an important engine to pass down ancient culture, enrich peasants and promote rural economic transition and upgrading. 现如今,乡村旅游已成为传承传统文化、提高农民收入、优化农村产业结构、促进农村经济转型的重要动力。

Health and Wellness Tourism

With the continuous development of the tourism industry, tourism has transformed from the basic "sightseeing tour" through to entertainment and sports tourism for the main purpose of health promotion, becoming a new direction of development in the tourism industry. Against this backdrop, health and wellness tourism has surged in China.①

Health and wellness tourism is a relatively new concept and field in Chinese tourism market. Health and wellness tourism can be described as a journey undertaken by people whose main motive is to preserve or promote their health and wellbeing.② And its essence is "an internal journey within oneself" for the purpose of finding, nurturing or healing.③ "Wellbeing holidays" are popular, because unlike normal holidays, there is less focus on family, children, or other ancillary arrangements. The focus is on "me". Indulgence, nurturing, and taking time off are among the main reasons for taking a wellness holiday.④

Health and wellness tourism as a whole can be divided into two categories: wellness tourism and medical tourism.

Wellness tourism is travel for the purpose of promoting health and well-being through physical, psychological, spiritual, or emotional activities such as yoga, meditation and spa treatment. Spa tourism is the best known form, focusing on the relaxation or healing of the body by way of water-based treatment, examples being: mineral or thermal pools, steam rooms, and saunas, with emphasis tending towards cure, rehabilitation, or rest.

Contemporarily, spas are well-established in China's larger cities. First-tier cities, notably Shanghai and Beijing, are replete with such offerings, and rumors of saturation are beginning to appear.⑤ With five-star hotels now looking further afield to second- and third-tier cities, international-standard hotel-based wellness facilities will likely extend their products more deeply into China in the very near future.

Vocabulary

ancillary 辅助的,附属的
indulgence 纵容,迁就
meditation 冥想
thermal 温热的,热量的
sauna 桑拿浴
rehabilitation 康复,修复
first-tier 一线的
saturation 饱和

实 用 导 游 英 语

Medical tourism can be defined as travel to destinations to undergo medical treatments such as surgery or other specialist interventions. However, medical tourism can have two major forms: surgical-involving operations, and therapeutic-undergoing healing treatments. In recent years, owing to the popularity of Chinese acupuncture, herbal medicine, Qi-Gong and shadow boxing⑥, medical tourism has sprouted worldwide.

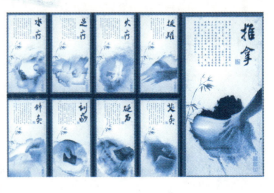

China has a number of destinations that fit the "Medical tourism" profile.⑦ Given a long history and its association with traditional Chinese medicine, a wealth of mountains and villages, multitudes of historical sites, and its status as an emerging and largely unexplored destination, China has the required ingredients to become a significant destination for Health and Wellness Tourism.⑧ Such a setting is ideal for the development of wellness resorts, which are still relatively rare in China. Without a doubt, China has a huge opportunity available, should it wish to tap into the rich and growing global health and wellness market.

intervention 干预,干涉
surgical 外科手术的
therapeutic 治疗的,疗法的

Notes

1. Against this backdrop, health and wellness tourism has surged in China. 在此背景下,中国的养生旅游产业应运而生。
2. Health and wellness tourism can be described as a journey undertaken by people whose main motive is to preserve or promote their health and wellbeing. 养生旅游是人们进行的一种旅行活动,其主要动机是保持或促进身体健康。
3. And its essence is "an internal journey within oneself" for the purpose of finding, nurturing or healing. 养生旅游的实质是"发现、滋养和治疗人们身心的一种内在旅行"。
4. Indulgence, nurturing, and taking time off are among the main reasons for taking a wellness holiday. 放纵、滋养和放松是人们选择养生旅游的几大主要原因。
5. First-tier cities, notably Shanghai and Beijing, are replete with such offerings, and rumors of saturation are beginning to appear. 在一线城市,尤其是北京和上海,水疗服务中心已是遍地开花,已经有议论说这些城市将很快出现饱和局面。
6. owing to the popularity of Chinese acupuncture, herbal medicine, Qi-Gong and shadow boxing 随着中国的针灸、中草药、气功和太极拳的流行
7. China has a number of destinations that fit the "Medical tourism" profile. 中国有很多地方适合发展养

生旅游。

8. Given a long history and its association with traditional Chinese medicine, a wealth of mountains and villages, multitudes of historical sites, and its status as an emerging and largely unexplored destination, China has the required ingredients to become a significant destination for Health and Wellness Tourism. 它的历史悠久，中医技术源远流长，山川村庄星罗棋布，历史名胜俯拾皆是。作为一个新兴的、有待开发的大市场，中国具备了成长为养生旅游者所追求的目的地的原始条件。

Useful Phrases and Expressions

1. patriotic education 爱国主义教育
2. holy land 圣地
3. sustainable development 可持续发展
4. be consistent with 与……一致
5. be classified into 分类为……
6. folk custom village 民俗村
7. ethnic minorities 少数民族

Exercises

Part I Listening Practice

Passage 1

The Reform of Education in a Mountainous Village in Shaanxi

integrate 整合
destitution 穷困，贫乏
barren 贫瘠的
test-oriented 以考试为目的的
occur to 想起，发生
verge 边缘
yield 产出，产量

实 用 导 游 英 语

Task 1 Listen to the passage carefully and then fill in the blanks with what you hear. The passage will be read only once.

People living in a _____1_____ mountainous area in Shaanxi Province have found a way to integrate the local school with the village, _____2_____ much needed farming skills and techniques.

For most of us, it may never occur that there are still people suffering from destitution and _____3_____ on the verge of poverty. But there are indeed such people, especially those living in mountainous areas of China, who are desperately trying to set out on the road of _____4_____. Barren land, together with a lack of knowledge, made it impossible for farmers to harvest yields. For years, hard work has brought the local people hardly enough to eat.

But in some villages, the most eye-catching _____5_____ is the teaching building of the village school. Villagers hope that their children can help the village _____6_____ poverty after they have gained knowledge. But many years had passed, the village was still poor. The reason is that the education mode is _____7_____ to be test-oriented, the key to which is to help students further their learning in advanced schools rather than for those who cannot enter higher schools. That's why students are not _____8_____ prepared to engage in farming; neither do they have the technical _____9_____ to do so. In order for the students to know more about basic farming skills, students in primary and junior high schools are all offered _____10_____ courses. And the students may choose different subjects according to their own interests. Students all feel that the courses are useful.

Task 2 Listen to the recording again and then answer the following questions.

(1) What happened in a mountainous village in Shaanxi Province?

_____

(2) What are the people living in the mountainous areas trying to do?

_____

(3) Why do the villagers send their children to the school?

_____

(4) Why can't the school education help the villagers shake off poverty?

(5) What did they do to reform local education? Is the reform fruitful?

Passage 2

Great Changes in Teaching Staff in China

> show up 出现
> unremitting 不懈的
> foremost 最重要的
> Ph.D 博士学位
> administrative 行政的
> replenish 补充
> properly 正确地

Task 1 Listen to the passage carefully and then fill in the blanks with what you hear. The passage will be read only once.

For a long time, the problems of retiring, lacking young teachers and low ____1____ of some teachers have obviously shown up concerning the teaching staff in China. To change the situation, ____2____ administrative departments at various levels made different policies and took all kinds of measures. After ten-year unremitting efforts, all those problems have been solved ____3____.

With many young teachers replenished, first and foremost, the age ____4____ of teachers' staff has been properly adjusted to a certain degree. A number of middle-aged and young teachers have ____5____ developed themselves and become the ____6____ teams in teaching and research.

As for the school administrators, they execute the policies relative to position ____7____ according to the performance and achievement of the teachers both in their teaching and in their ____8____ work. The proportion of teachers who have Ph. D and master's degree has been increased so that the degree structure of teachers has been more ____9____. At the same time, further education is provided for those excellent teachers. They can either go aboard for advanced studies or carry out ____10____ research with the experts in university.

Task 2   Have you got a clear idea about the changes taken place in the field of education in the last ten-year period? Try to describe these changes without looking at the passage.

Part II Oral Practice

Task 1   Group Discussion

Divide the class into small groups and each student will give his/her group member a summary of the emerging tourism mentioned in the texts. Then ask other students to make some additions if necessary.

Task 2   Role Play

Work in groups of 4 or 5. One of you is a tour guide. The rest are foreign visitors. The guide is taking the visitors around the ancient city of Wuzhen. The guide is introducing Chinese traditional architecture, lifestyle and crafts to them.

Part III Translation

Task 1   Translate the following words or phrases into English

(1) 革命遗址
(2) 爱国主义教育
(3) 中国共产党的成立
(4) 与……相联系
(5) 毛主席故居
(6) 八一南昌起义
(7) 民俗村
(8) 亲身体验
(9) 城市的喧嚣
(10) 二三线城市

Unit 13 Emerging Tourism

Task 2   Translate the following paragraph into English.

乡村旅游的显著特点在于:其初衷是要让游客享受个性化的接触,体验乡村的自然环境和人文氛围,并且尽量让游客参与当地人的活动,感受其传统风俗和生活方式。据估计(estimate),在跨国旅游中,乡村旅游占3%。并且乡村旅游的年均增长率约达6%,比整个旅游业的年均增幅高出两个百分点(percentage points)。由此可见,乡村旅游拥有巨大的潜在市场。

Task 3   Translate the following paragraph into Chinese.

The growth of medical and wellness tourism is believed to be long-lasting. There are many factors converging to drive growth: the swelling population of aging Baby Boomers; increased stress in people's lives, necessitating a sharper focus on wellness and especially prevention; and improved technology, which is not only delivering more medical and health options, but also the ability to learn about travel offerings around the globe, especially via the Internet.

导游技巧和业务
Professional Tour Guiding Knowledge & Skills

新旅游法

为整顿和规范旅游市场,维护旅游者的权益,促进旅游业的全面协调、可持续发展,《中华人民共和国旅游法》经2013年4月25日十二届全国人大常委会第2次会议通过,于2013年10月1日起施行。新旅游法主要关注以下十大焦点问题。

倡导文明出游
- 第十三条:旅游者在旅游活动中应当遵守社会公共秩序和社会公德,尊重当地的风俗习惯、文化传统和宗教信仰,爱护旅游资源,保护生态环境,遵守旅游文明行为规范。

保护旅游资源 (tourism resource)
- 第二十一条:对自然资源和文物等人文资源进行旅游利用,必须严格遵守有关法律、法规,符合资源、生态保护和文物安全的要求,尊重和维护当地传统文化和习俗,维护

实用导游英语

资源的区域整体性、文化代表性和地域特殊性,并考虑军事设施保护的需要。

规范"一日游"

- 第二十六条:旅游主管部门和地方政府应当根据需要,建立旅游公共信息和咨询平台,无偿向旅游者提供旅游景区、线路、交通、气象、住宿、安全、医疗急救等必要信息和咨询服务。

禁止"零负团费",取消自费项目 (zero-or-negative-fare tours)

- 第三十五条:旅行社不得以不合理的低价组织旅游活动,并通过安排购物或者另行付费旅游项目获取回扣;不得指定具体购物场所,不得安排另行付费旅游项目(经双方协商一致或者旅游者要求,且不影响其他旅游者行程安排的除外)。

不得索要小费、回扣 (kickback)

- 第四十一条:导游和领队应当严格执行旅游行程安排,不得擅自变更旅游行程或者中止服务活动,不得向旅游者索取小费,不得诱导、欺骗、强迫或者变相强迫旅游者购物或者参加另行付费的旅游项目。

规范景区门票价格

- 第四十三条:严格控制价格上涨,景区提高门票价格应当提前六个月公布,涨价应举行听证会(出席人员须含旅游者);公益性景区应逐步免费开放。

禁止景区超载接待游客

- 第四十五条:景区接待旅游者不得超过景区主管部门核定的最大承载量。制定和实施旅游者流量控制方案(可采取门票预约等方式)。

不可抗力责任分担

- 第六十七条:合同不能继续履行的,旅行社和旅游者均可以解除合同。合同解除的,将余款退还旅游者;危及旅游者人身、财产安全的,旅行社应当采取相应的安全措施,因此支出的费用,由旅行社与旅游者分担。

旅游安全及救援
- 第八十一条:突发事件或者旅游安全事故发生后,旅游经营者应当立即采取必要的救助和处置措施,依法履行报告义务,并对旅游者作出妥善安排。
- 第八十二条:旅游者在人身、财产安全遇有危险时,有权请求旅游经营者、当地政府和相关机构进行及时救助。

及时处理游客投诉
- 第九十一条:县级以上人民政府应当指定或者设立统一的旅游投诉受理机构。受理机构接到投诉,应当及时进行处理或者移交有关部门处理,并告知投诉者。

小贴士

中国公民出境旅游文明行为指南
- 中国公民,出境旅游,注重礼仪,保持尊严。
- 讲究卫生,爱护环境;衣着得体,请勿喧哗。
- 尊老爱幼,助人为乐;女士优先,礼貌谦让。
- 出行办事,遵守时间;排队有序,不越黄线。
- 文明住宿,不损用品;安静用餐,请勿浪费。
- 健康娱乐,有益身心;赌博色情,坚决拒绝。
- 参观游览,遵守规定;习俗禁忌,切勿冒犯。
- 遇有疑难,咨询领馆;文明出行,一路平安。

Discussion & Exercise

Task 1　What is the significance of the new Tourism Law?

Task 2　What are the main issues the new Tourism Law aims to solve?

Task 3　Complete the following sentences by translating the Chinese in the brackets into English.

1. Over the past 30 years, tourism has gradually grown into a _____ (支柱产业) of the national economy in China.

2. New Tourism Law shall _____ (开始实施) on October 1, 2013.
3. The new law will inevitably _____ (引发旅游市场重新洗牌).
4. The travel agencies have _____ (调整业务) according to the rules stipulated in the law.
5. It requires travel agencies to use _____ (产品的创新和优质的服务), instead of tempting prices, to attract customers.
6. The new law bans the rampant practice of "_____ (零负团费)" in the country, which refers to tour services sold by travel agents at or below cost in order to attract travellers, who are later forced to purchase goods or tip agents during their tours.
7. The new law also outlined measures to address key problems, _____ (不正当竞争、肆意涨价、景区拥挤), which have plagued the industry and aroused strong public discontent.
8. The Tourism Law is designed to address industry woes, protect tourists' interests, and _____ (促进旅游业可持续发展).

Case Study

Recent years have witnessed a dramatic growth in China's tourism. Along with it comes a surge in criticism of the way some Chinese tourists behave, such as queue jumping, spitting or littering on the ground and even carving characters on cultural relics. These uncivilized behaviors have seriously damaged the ecological environment, tourism resources and also the country's image.

Questions

1. What are the regulations concerning tourists' behavior according to the new Tourism Law?
2. What proper behavior should the tour leader tell the group heading abroad?

1. 红色延安
2. 生态黄河
3. 民俗大观——十二生肖

练习参考答案

Unit 1

Part I
Passage 1, Task 1

1. attract tourists back
2. 20 consecutive
3. a dramatic drop
4. 6.97 billion Yuan
5. discounts
6. tour operators
7. stands of wondrous caves
8. off-season policy
9. 120 Yuan
10. outbreak

Passage 2, Task 1

1. pegged
2. a positive effect
3. tourism industry
4. 600
5. 10,657 Yuan
6. lower price
7. shopping activities
8. 20%
9. inbound tours
10. relatively stable

Part III Translation
Task 1

1. a vast territory with abundant resources
2. co-prosperity
3. rich in products
4. an inspiring place producing outstanding people
5. sustainable development
6. population density
7. preferential policy
8. Mt. Everest
9. National Population Census
10. a united multi-ethnic country

Task 2

Since 1970s, the Chinese government has made unremitting efforts to implement the basic state policy of family planning all over the country. It has encouraged late marriage and late childbearing, and advocated only one child for each couple. Owing to the strenuous hard work in the past thirty years, China has effectively controlled the over-rapid population growth while the national economy still remains undeveloped, and realized the historical change in the population reproduction type to the one characterized by low birth and death rates and a slow natural population growth rate. This situation has enhanced China's overall national power, advanced the society, and improved peoples' lives. China has made active contributions to stabilizing the world's population.

Task 3

中国横贯东亚大陆,东西长约5,026公里,濒临东海、黄海和南海,位于朝鲜和越南之间,地形多变,拥有广阔的平原、浩瀚的沙漠和巍峨的山脉,包括大量无人荒地。

导游技巧和业务 Task 3

1. ensure that everything goes smoothly
2. demands tact and diplomacy
3. the tourist's inquiries
4. an atmosphere of teamwork
5. call the tourist's name whenever possible
6. Escorting tourists
7. an integral part of a successful tour
8. be aware of what is next on the itinerary

Unit 2

Part I
Passage 1, Task 1

1. evil spirits
2. evolved
3. Halloween color
4. jack-o'lanterns
5. miser
6. the devil
7. Judgment Day
8. windows of a house
9. goodies
10. Trick or Treat

Passage 2, Task 1

1. promote
2. controversy
3. pilot program
4. unique cultural treasures
5. 200
6. poll
7. 38
8. compulsory
9. local operas
10. reservoir

Part III Translation
Task 1

1. fireworks and firecrackers
2. reunion dinner
3. dragon dance and lion dance
4. lantern exhibits and riddles
5. get rid of ill fortune
6. paper cuts
7. Spring Festival paintings
8. to bid farewell to old year
9. to have a toast
10. to give New Year greetings

Task 2

The ninth day of the ninth lunar month is a very important traditional festival for Chinese called Chongyangjie festival with a history of 2,000 years. The Chinese government decreed the day as Seniors' Day in 1989, so local governments organize activities for senior citizens such as mountain climbing and autumn outings on that day to help them communicate with the outside world and get some exercise. A great many juniors go picnicking with their parents and grandparents on the day, too. The traditional activities on the day include outings, mountain climbing, enjoying the chrysanthemum blossoms and cornel planting.

Task 3

现在,每年正月十五,中国各地仍然把举办灯会看成是件大事。人们尽情享受灯火辉煌的夜晚。就拿中国西南的四川省成都市来说吧,每年该市都在文化公园举办灯会。在元宵节期间,整个公园简直就是一片灯海。新颖的设计吸引着无数游人。最引人注目的当属龙柱灯,只见一条金龙盘旋在27米高度柱子上,口中吐出焰火。其景象十分壮观。

导游技巧和业务　Task 3

1. taboo
2. tactics/diplomacy
3. delaying tactics
4. subtle
5. disabled tourists
6. religious beliefs
7. careful preparations are required
8. face to face confrontations

Unit 3

Part I
Passage 1, Task 1

1. nationwide
2. estimated
3. command

4. second-tier	5. acceleration	6. felt
7. launched	8. agents	9. volume
10. polled		

Passage 2, Task 1

1. consultant	2. potential	3. unique
4. passed	5. which	6. attached
7. financial	8. new-emerging	9. showcase
10. committed		

Part III Translation
Task 1

1. international exchange	2. cultural content
3. mongolian yurt	4. grand gathering
5. propose a toast to	6. folk custom
7. extend a warm welcome to	8. distinguished guest
9. host a series of events	10. non-renewable resource

Task 2

The Water Splashing Festival is a ceremony celebrated by the De'ang people during the New Year and provides an opportunity for the boys and girls to scope out their lovers. Sending the bamboo basket late at night to express their love to their beloved girls is popular among the De'ang people. Hence, every girl can get several baskets. But the final lover is determined at the Water Splashing Festival depending on whose basket the girl will carry.

Task 3

冰雕是采用冰作为原料的一种雕塑形式。由于冰材料的变化性和易挥发性,冰的雕刻有诸多困难。冰必须精心挑选,以宜于雕塑。理想的冰材料应该由纯净的水制成,这样的冰透明度高。而且好冰所含的气泡是最少的。

导游技巧和业务   Task 3

1. the method of Question-and-Answer Introduction
2. a Section-by-Section Explanatory Introduction
3. the Introduction with a Focus on Key Events

4. narrate in a matter-of-fact manner

5. draw an analogy

6. the method of Leading Someone to a Fascinating Vista

7. Giving a Crucial Touch to a Picture

8. creating suspension

Unit 4

Part I
Passage 1, Task 1

1. underdeveloped	2. rise	3. loyalty
4. sites	5. generated	6. supposed
7. either	8. economic	9. memorials
10. connecting		

Passage 2, Task 1

1. approved	2. role	3. bilateral
4. source	5. up	6. account
7. appeals	8. yet	9. further
10. Administration		

Part III Translation
Task 1

1. sterilize	2. sidewalk food stall/sidewalk snack booth
3. hot pot/ instant-boiled mutton	4. regional cuisines
5. authentic Muslim food	6. imperial court dishes
7. local delicacies	8. ask for a doggy bag
9. medicinal diet	10. specialty

Task 2

Many foreigners are interested in but also puzzled about how to use chopsticks. First, hold the pair of chopsticks in the right hand, using the index finger, middle finger and ring finger to keep the chopsticks near their top and then push them open by moving the thumb and index finer. While eating, lift upward the top chopstick with the index and middle fingers and keep the bottom one stationary. Once food is picked up, press one of the chopsticks with the thumb and index finer and raise the pair.

Practice a lot and then you will find it is an easy job.

Task 3

中国药膳不是食物与中药的简单相加，而是在中医辨证配膳理论指导下，由药物、食物和调料三者精制而成。它既有药物功效，又有食品美味，用以防病治病、强身益寿的特殊食品。

中国药膳已经被世界所接受。近年来不少药膳罐头和中药保健饮料、药酒等已销往国际市场。

导游技巧和业务　Task 3

1. bungee jumping
2. drowning
3. a room with sea-view
4. the refund
5. reasonable requests
6. optional programs which are not included in the itinerary
7. relics
8. personal requests

Unit 5

Part I
Passage 1, Task 1

1. iconic   2. Harbor Bridge   3. full-sized   4. Buddha
5. attractions 6. tourist mecca   7. the Forbidden City
8. architectural style   9. functional halls   10. prosperity

Passage 2, Task 1

1. heaven   2. ornamental   3. lofts   4. paradise
5. galleries   6. art studios   7. dignitaries   8. celebrities
9. designated   10. platform

Part III Translation
Task 1

1. medicinal wine   2. alcohol content

3. cheers/bottoms up   4. hard liquor
5. propose for a toast   6. tea sets
7. sip tea   8. the picking season
9. get refreshed/ refresh yourself   10. Tea and Horse Road

Task 2

Tea culture is one of the common traits shared by all the 56 ethnic groups in China. Many Chinese people believe that a day is not perfect without a cup of tea. Either in the warm southern mountain areas or on the frozen northern grasslands, stuff like Gongfu tea, buttered tea and milk tea are all among the favorite drinks. Furthermore, both ancient and modern Chinese people tend to indulge in elaborating on poems, essays, dances and dramas on the tea.

Task 3

与西方的葡萄酒不同,中国酒是从大米、小米、其他粮食、药草和花中提炼的。各种各样的滋补酒是用传统原料制成的。深受欢迎的米酒黄酒最好是温着喝,黄酒的味道与中干的雪利酒相似,可以与很多中国菜搭配着喝,特别是在凉爽的季节。高粱酒和茅台酒是烈性酒,由小米提炼而成,酒精含量达到70%,最好在饭后喝。

导游技巧和业务 Task 3

1. nationality, occupation, age, gender and social status
2. are well educated
3. Elderly tourists
4. current affairs
5. the parking place and departure time
6. keep an eye on their children
7. Lady first
8. income, marital status, political orientation and religious belief

Unit 6

Part I
Passage 1, Task 1

1. ongoing   2. rarely have a touch   3. presented
4. accepted   5. northern China   6. elements

7. sold out   8. drew artists   9. assured
10. appreciate

Passage 2, Task 1

1. A Hundred Flowers in Bloom
2. November 11th to 18th
3. practitioners
4. 80%
5. travel packages
6. simultaneous interpretations
7. facing a challenge
8. entertainment
9. comeback
10. cultivate

Part III Translation

Task 1

1. delicate tune
2. elegant gesture
3. melodious voice of music
4. the quintessence of Chinese culture
5. blind and dazzle
6. play a blinder
7. special wonder
8. turn a somersault
9. diabolo
10. miracle

Task 2

After the stage practices of numerous performers for a long time, the stagecraft of Beijing Opera has formed a set of interactive and mutual beneficial rules and standards in stylization with respect to literature, performing, music, voicing, dressing and make-up. It has gone beyond the boundaries of the space and time within the stage and has reached the art perfection of "expressing the spirit through physical performance, while achieving the precision in both".

Task 3

从瓷花瓶、玻璃瓶到人，中国杂技可以利用任何道具来表演戏法，用长竿转碟子、叠罗汉、钻火圈。中国杂技的特色表演还包括走钢丝，演员们可以在钢索上翻跟头、表演跳板杂技以及"爬高竿"，杂技演员要在高竿上保持平衡的同时做各种特技表演。

导游技巧和业务　Task 3

1. unpredictable accidents
2. emergency situations
3. emergency procedure manual
4. the missing tourists
5. tsunami
6. as far as the tourists' safety is concerned

7. shark attacks   8. landslides/mudslides

Unit 7

Part I
Passage 1, Task 1
1. appreciation
2. positive
3. overseas
4. immediately
5. local shopping
6. continuing rise
7. revaluation
8. overall
9. market
10. tourism-related

Passage 2, Task 1
1. striking and convincing
2. doctorate degree
3. diploma
4. college education
5. races and genders
6. widened
7. weight
8. tobacco use
9. trend
10. deaths

Part III Translation
Task 1
1. mixed-use complex
2. a building of brick and wood
3. encircling wall
4. sculptural decorations
5. well-ventilated
6. French window
7. vault-like construction
8. technical brilliance
9. sound insulation
10. perfect contrast

Task 2
The earth towers of Hakka, the unparalleled legendary of villagers' residences, are a pearl of eastern culture, and an exotic flower in Chinese architectural history. The towers have long been famous in world architecture, due to their long history, unique designation, magnificent style and delicate structure. Besides being able to resist long sieges, the towers are secure against earthquakes, fires and bandits. They can also boast having good ventilation and lighting. Due to the thick earth walls, the towers are well insulated so as keep people cool during the summer and warm during the winter.

Task 3

建筑和文化息息相关。在某种程度上,建筑是文化的载体。中国许多古建筑都包括一个小庭院。与西方教堂所追求的多维空间的理念不同,古代中国人所设计的房屋更适合人类本身的诉求,这样人们才能体会到彼此之间的亲密,才会感到安全。而这种思想恰恰体现了中国文化的实用思想。

导游技巧和业务   Task 3

1. make a complaint
2. claims
3. satisfactory resolution
4. regulatory agencies
5. look into the matter
6. the inconvenience
7. attend to it/the matter
8. sincere apologies

Unit 8

Part I
Passage 1, Task 1

1. aspects
2. characteristics
3. currently
4. better
5. nature
6. Buddhism
7. basically
8. existence
9. positive
10. celebrates

Passage 2, Task 1

1. dramatically
2. contradictions
3. localization
4. established
5. superiority
6. literature
7. prose
8. merits
9. chemistry
10. philosophic

Part III Translation
Task 1

1. religion belief
2. enlightenment
3. immortal being
4. Confucianism
5. take the elixir
6. prophet
7. monotheism
8. Buddhism sutras
9. De
10. become God when they have Dao

Task 2

Among the three religions in China, Confucianism and Taoism are genuinely Chinese religion, while Buddhism is derived from India. However, under the great influence of China's policy, these three religions have formed a harmonious and beneficial co-existence, which constitutes a glorious and splendid Chinese culture and meanwhile makes irreplaceable contributions to human civilization and ideology.

Task 3

所有的宗教,不管大小,必须适应一个完全不同于它们所产生时的世界。现世主义和科学发挥着重大的作用,虽然这些作用更多体现在发达国家而非发展中国家。尽管科学在某些方面可能会弱化宗教,但是它也为传播宗教创造新的机会。

导游技巧和业务　Task 3

1. the Communist Party of China
2. flag raising ceremony
3. the military band
4. National Anthem
5. The national emblem
6. the China's Tourism Emblem
7. at sunrise
8. Tian'anmen Rostrum

Unit 9

Part I
Passage 1, Task 1

1. classical
2. martial
3. performed
4. worshipped
5. trace
6. indirect
7. meditation
8. animals
9. combat
10. defend

Passage 2, Task 1

1. pressures
2. lifestyle
3. medical
4. equally
5. emotions
6. restore
7. maintain
8. established
9. popularity
10. herbal

Part III Translation

Task 1

1. *Yellow Emperor's Classic of Internal Medicine*
2. take their patients' pulses
3. meridian
4. balance between Yin and Yang
5. chronic diseases
6. climatic changes
7. inspection, smelling, inquiry and palpation
8. complexion
9. Chinese herbal medicine
10. well-being and happiness

Task 2

Hua Tuo is considered a divine doctor and is worshiped as a medicinal god. "Hua Tuo Reincarnated" is a term of respect for a highly skilled doctor. Therapies and body-building methods created by Hua Tuo are significant milestones in Chinese medical history. Hua Tuo was thereby respectfully called "Originator of Surgery" by later generations.

Task 3

有历史记载的最早发现并诊断治疗的案例可以追溯到公元前1500年,大概在中国商代时期。中国早期医学的哲学根据似乎是在寻求一种生者与他们死去的祖先以及地球上善灵与恶灵之间的和谐。

导游技巧和业务   Task 3

1. customs form	2. chartered flights	3. bad weather
4. compensation	5. is now boarding	6. force majeure
7. carrying luggage	8. security check	

Unit 10

Part I
Passage 1, Task 1

1. collapsed
2. split
3. cover
4. the weak and the old
5. colors
6. turtle
7. ashes
8. tamed
9. dome
10. benefited

Passage 2, Task 1

1. universally
2. foundations
3. expression
4. subject
5. separation
6. obstacles
7. conform
8. distinctive
9. heroes
10. supernatural

Part III Translation
Task 1

1. Cowherd and Weaving Girl
2. celestial princess
3. Silvery River
4. magpie bridge
5. state funeral
6. an earthly life
7. Divine Couple
8. an earthly mortal
9. Jade Emperor
10. rising upwards towards the sky

Task 2

Journey to the West, as one of China's Four Classics, is a very popular folk story in China. It tells that Tang Priest XuanZang journeyed west with his three disciples, overcoming all kinds of difficulties to attain Buddhism Sutras and then fulfilled his mission at last. In this book, the clever and brave monkey—Sun Wukong, the lazy and greedy pig—Zhu Wuneng and the hard-working and responsible monk—Sha Wujin all leave a deep impression on the readers.

Task 3

在黄金时代,地球上最初有了定居者。这是一个天真无邪和幸福的时代。真理和正义主宰着一切,不是依靠法律的约束,也没有什么权贵的统治和惩罚。人们不需要耕种,生活所需的一切东西都可以从大地中获得。

导游技巧和业务　Task 3

1. the Ministry of Foreign Affairs
2. tourist visa
3. group visa
4. had expired
5. the regulations of entry and exit
6. declared to the Customs Office
7. criminal records
8. visas on arrival

Unit 11

Part I
Passage 1, Task 1

1. scope
2. platform
3. reinforcing
4. sharp
5. Benefiting
6. exploration
7. given
8. adopt
9. secondary
10. enrollment

Passage 2, Task 1

1. military
2. patterned
3. finalized
4. reign
5. subsequent
6. vertical
7. borderline
8. circles
9. manuals
10. popularizing

Part III Translation
Task 1

1. Chinese civilization
2. four treasures of the study
3. the four arts of the well-bred
4. combination with mobility and immobility
5. build up a strong constitution
6. military strategy
7. gambling
8. world championship
9. mental challenge
10. internal temperament

Task 2

The Chinese knot is a special Chinese folk manual technique, with its unique art of Oriental verve, colorful change, fully embodies the wisdom of the Chinese people and the profound cultural connotation. The Chinese knot is a knot with 13 basic knots. The arbitrary combinations of the 13 basic knots can create a great number of beautiful crafts.

Task 3

现代的筷子上有可能会有你的星座（无论是西方还是东方），各种季节的花草或者动物，还或者是流行的卡通角色。有一些商店对筷子的销售做出了极大的贡献，在这样的商店中，你可以看到各式各样的用来吃饭的筷子，无论是细尖的用来吃鱼的筷子还是那种用来吃意大利面的螺旋形的筷子，抑或是那种底部像勺子一样用来吃茶泡饭的筷子。

导游技巧和业务　Task 3

1. by credit card
2. foreign currencies
3. traveler's checks
4. merchant commission
5. American Express
6. exchange rate
7. valid
8. exchange memo

Unit 12

Part I
Passage 1, Task 1

1. paid
2. opt
3. adventurous
4. active
5. presented
6. allowed
7. prefer
8. fulfilled
9. alive
10. emerging

Passage 2, Task 1

1. primary motivation
2. forms of tourism
3. mass tourism
4. caters to
5. undertaken
6. relevant
7. consists of
8. individualized
9. range from
10. resorts

Part III Translation

Task 1

1. whitewater rafting
2. indigenous people
3. local tourism administrations
4. wildlife spectacle
5. terraced fields
6. picturesque Guilin
7. home and abroad
8. local specialties
9. mysterious lure
10. the quintessence of culture

Task 2

Bicycle touring generally means self-contained cycling trips over long distances, which prioritize pleasure, adventure and autonomy rather than sport, commuting or exercise. Tours may be planned and organized by the participants themselves or organized for a group by a professional holiday business, or a club. Bicycle touring can be of any time and distances vary considerably. Depending on fitness, speed and the number of stops, the rider usually covers between 50—150 kilometres (30—90 mi) per day. A short tour over a few days may cover as little as 200 kilometres (120 mi) and a long tour may go right across a country or around the world.

Task 3

简而言之，背包旅游是一种独立、经济且经常跨国界的旅行方式。背包旅行时，人们使用便于长途和长时间携带的背包或其他行李，住宿便宜，如选择青年旅舍。通常是年轻人背包旅游，他们一般义务负担不多，因此有更多的时间旅游。背包徒步旅行的人被称为"背包客"。比起其他旅行者，背包客通常旅行时间更长，并走出国门到几个不同的国家体验当地风俗民情和饱览风景名胜。

导游技巧和业务　Task 3

1. etiquette
2. openly accept compliments
3. auspicious creature
4. celebrations and joyful occasions
5. Taboo
6. euphemism
7. straightforward
8. body language

Unit 13

Part I
Passage 1, Task 1

1. poverty-stricken
2. offering
3. struggling
4. prosperity
5. construction
6. shake off
7. designed
8. psychologically
9. know-how
10. relevant

Passage 2, Task 1

1. qualification
2. educational
3. primarily
4. structure
5. gradually
6. backbone
7. promotion
8. research
9. adjusted
10. cooperative

Part III Translation
Task 1

1. revolutionary sites
2. patriotic education
3. the founding of the Communist Party of China
4. be associated with
5. Former Residence of Chairman Mao
6. August 1, 1927, Nanchang Uprising
7. folk custom village
8. a hands-on experience
9. hustle and bustle of the city
10. second- and third-tier cities

Task 2

The distinguishing feature of tourism products in rural tourism is the wish to give visitors a personalized experience, a taste of the physical and human environment of the countryside and, as far as possible, allow them to participate in the activities, traditions and lifestyles of local people. It is estimated that three percent of all international tourists travel for rural tourism purposes and rural tourism is growing at an annual rate of around six percent, two percentage points above the growth rate for all tourism. From the above, we conclude that there is a high potential market for rural tourism.

Task 3

　　医疗和养生旅游的发展趋势必将是持久的。众多不同的因素将共同促进其向前发展，这些因素包括：婴儿潮时代出生的人逐渐老龄化；生活压力增大；人们对身心健康越来越重视，尤其是对预防疾病越来越重视；科学技术的不断发展，技术的发展不仅向人们提供了越来越多的医疗和健康选择，而且增进了人们对世界各地旅游项目的了解，尤其是通过互联网。

导游技巧和业务　　Task 3

1. pillar industry
2. come into effect
3. lead to a reshuffle of the tourism industry
4. adjusted their business operations
5. product innovation and high-quality service
6. zero- or negative-fare tours
7. unfair competition, wanton price hikes and congestion in scenic spots
8. foster the industry's sustainable growth

参考书目

Chen, Yu. Li, Guishan (translator). *Fascinating Mural Stories from Dunhuang Grottoes, vol. 2.* Beijing: New World Press, 2008.

Chung Mou Si. Yun Cheng Si. *Introduction to Chinese Culture.* Beijing: Peking University Press, 2011.

Low, Shawn. Harper, Damian. et al. *Lonely Planet China (Travel Guide),* Lonely Planet, 2013.

Qi, Xin. Miao, Ling (translator). *Chinese Festivals.* Beijing: Foreign Languages Press, 2008.

Stockwell, Foster. Tang, Bowen. Zuo, Boyang. *Recent discoveries in Chinese Archeology: 28 articles by Chinese archeologists describing their excavations.* Beijing: Foreign Languages Press, 1984.

Tour Guiding and Resort Representation by Scottish Qualifications Authority. Beijing: China Modern Economic Publishing House, 2004.

北京市旅游局：《导游业务》，北京：燕山出版社，2007年。
北京市旅游局导游资格考评委员会：《北京主要景点》，北京：北京燕山出版社，2009年。
常俊跃等主编：《中国文化（英文版）》，北京：北京大学出版社，2011年。
常宗林、李旭奎主编：《中国文化导读》，北京：清华大学出版社，2006年。
纪春、裴松青，《英语导游教程》，北京：旅游教育出版社，2007年。
国家旅游局人事劳动教育司：《导游业务》（第7版），北京：旅游教育出版社，2013年。
葛益娟、张骏主编：《导游实务》，北京：旅游教育出版社，2010年。
黄向、苏丹编著：《旅游英语》，广州：暨南大学出版社，2009年。
教育部《旅游英语》教材编写组：《旅游英语》，北京：高等教育出版社，2008年。
柯淑萍、孙培主编：《饭店英语听说教程》，杭州：浙江大学出版社，2008年。
李海玲：《导游带团技能速成——经典案例训练》，北京：中国旅游出版社，2013年。
王君、冯海霞：《景区景点实用英语》，北京：旅游教育出版社，2007年。
云南省人民政府新闻办公室：《云南：云天之外的香格里拉》，北京：外文出版社，2006年。
张玲敏主编：《导游英语360句》，北京：旅游教育出版社，2008年。
朱华：《英语导游实务教程》，北京：北京大学出版社，2012年。

China Travel Guide:http://www.travelchinaguide.com/
中国网：http://www.china.com.cn/
www.chinaculture.org
http://www.chinesefolkculture.com
http://www.china-fun.netl
http://www.hukoupubu.cc/
http://www.hgscn.com/
http://www.lnbxsd.com/
http://www.xinhuanet.com/english/

http://www.lonelyplanet.com
http://whc.unesco.org
http://docuchina.cntv.cn/
http://travel.cntv.cn/
http://www.bbc.co.uk/
http://ngm.nationalgeographic.com/
http://dsc.discovery.com/
http://www.cnadventure.com/index.htm
http://www.chinaculturecenter.org/
http://baike.baidu.com
http://knowledge.sagepub.com
http://www.chinaodysseytours.com
www.acupuncturechinanawei.com
http://apps.cctv.com/english/TouchChina
www.baidu.com
www.bbc.co.uk
www.c-c-c.org/chineseculture/festival/dragonboat/dragon.html
http://chinatravelz.com
http://www.chinahotelsreservation.com
www.chinesefortunecalendar.com
http://cn.macautourism.gov.mo/gb/index.php
http://www.cnwh.org
http://www.dunhuangtour.com
http://en.wikipedia.org/wiki
http://en.w
http://en.summerpalace-china.com
http://english.china.com
http://www.eng.taoism.org.
http://eedu.org.cn
www.healthy.net
http://www.hkta.org
http://www.mount-tai.com.cn
http://news.xinhuanet.com
www.religioustolerance.org
www.religioustolerance.org
http://www.sacred-destinations.com

《实用导游英语》

尊敬的老师:

您好!

为了方便您更好地使用本教材,获得最佳教学效果,我们特向使用该书作为教材的教师赠送本教材配套听力资料。如有需要,请完整填写"教师联系表"并加盖所在单位系(院)公章,免费向出版社索取。

北京大学出版社

教 师 联 系 表

教材名称	《实用导游英语》		
姓名:	性别:	职务:	职称:
E-mail:	联系电话:	邮政编码:	
供职学校:	所在院系:		(章)
学校地址:			
教学科目与年级:	班级人数:		
通信地址:			

填写完毕后,请将此表邮寄给我们,我们将为您免费寄送本教材配套资料,谢谢!

北京市海淀区成府路205号
北京大学出版社外语编辑部　刘　爽
邮政编码:100871
电子邮箱:nkliushuang@hotmail.com

邮 购 部 电 话:010-62534449
市场营销部电话:010-62750672
外语编辑部电话:010-62759634